BELLINGHAM
5

adidas
BoyleSports
THIS IS BETTING.

JUDE BELLINGHAM

FOOTBALL FAN BOOK

TEAMS · GOALS · SUPERSTAR

WRITTEN BY IAIN SPRAGG

sona BOOKS

First published in the UK by Sona Books, an imprint of Danann Media Publishing Limited

CAT NO: SON0625

Photography courtesy of

Getty images, Alamy and Wiki Commons

Project editor: Martin Corteel

Book layout & design: Kevin Gardner

Proofreader: Cameron Thurlow

Printed in EU.

ISBN: 978-1-915343-92-5

CONTENTS

INTRODUCTION

By the time most aspiring footballers, however talented, celebrate their 21st birthday they are dreaming of breaking into their club's first team and, perhaps, one day playing for their country.

When Jude Bellingham marked the same milestone, he had already played professionally in three of Europe's top five leagues – England, Germany and Spain – and was already a veteran of three major international tournaments with England.

Football has heralded countless young stars before but in Bellingham the beautiful game has unearthed a player of rare quality.

The sporting story of the boy from the Midlands is as remarkable as it has been played out at breakneck speed. A senior player with first club Birmingham City at the age of just 16, he took the bold decision to move abroad while still a teenager and pursue his footballing education in the unfamiliar surroundings of Germany with Borussia Dortmund.

It was an audacious gamble so early in his embryonic career but one which paid off spectacularly and in his three seasons of service in the Bundesliga, he was irrepressible, maturing into a polished midfielder of undoubted class, guile and power.

His displays for Dortmund earned him a dream move to Real Madrid in the summer of 2023 and Bellingham proved to be to the manor born instantly in Spain. In his first season at the Bernabéu the young English star was pivotal as Los Blancos claimed a coveted double, winning La Liga and the Champions League.

For England he quickly emerged as no less talismanic. Debuting for the Three Lions as a 17-year-old under Gareth Southgate in 2020, he already has two Euro campaigns and a World Cup on his burgeoning CV and

yet to reach the peak of his tactical or physical powers, the best is surely yet to come for club and country.

Football has heralded countless young stars before but in Bellingham the beautiful game has unearthed a player of rare quality with longevity, natural talent and relentless dedication and, most excitingly, that elusive ability to produce magic moments at the most critical and dramatic of times. Bellingham became a star at a ridiculously early age but his incredible trajectory is still firmly on the up.

ABOVE: Bellingham's trademark goal celebration is already iconic.

THE EARLY YEARS

A SUPERSTAR-IN-WAITING FROM CHILDHOOD, JUDE BELLINGHAM'S JUNIOR CAREER MARKED HIM OUT AS A PLAYER WITH THE POTENTIAL TO SUCCEED AT THE HIGHEST LEVEL.

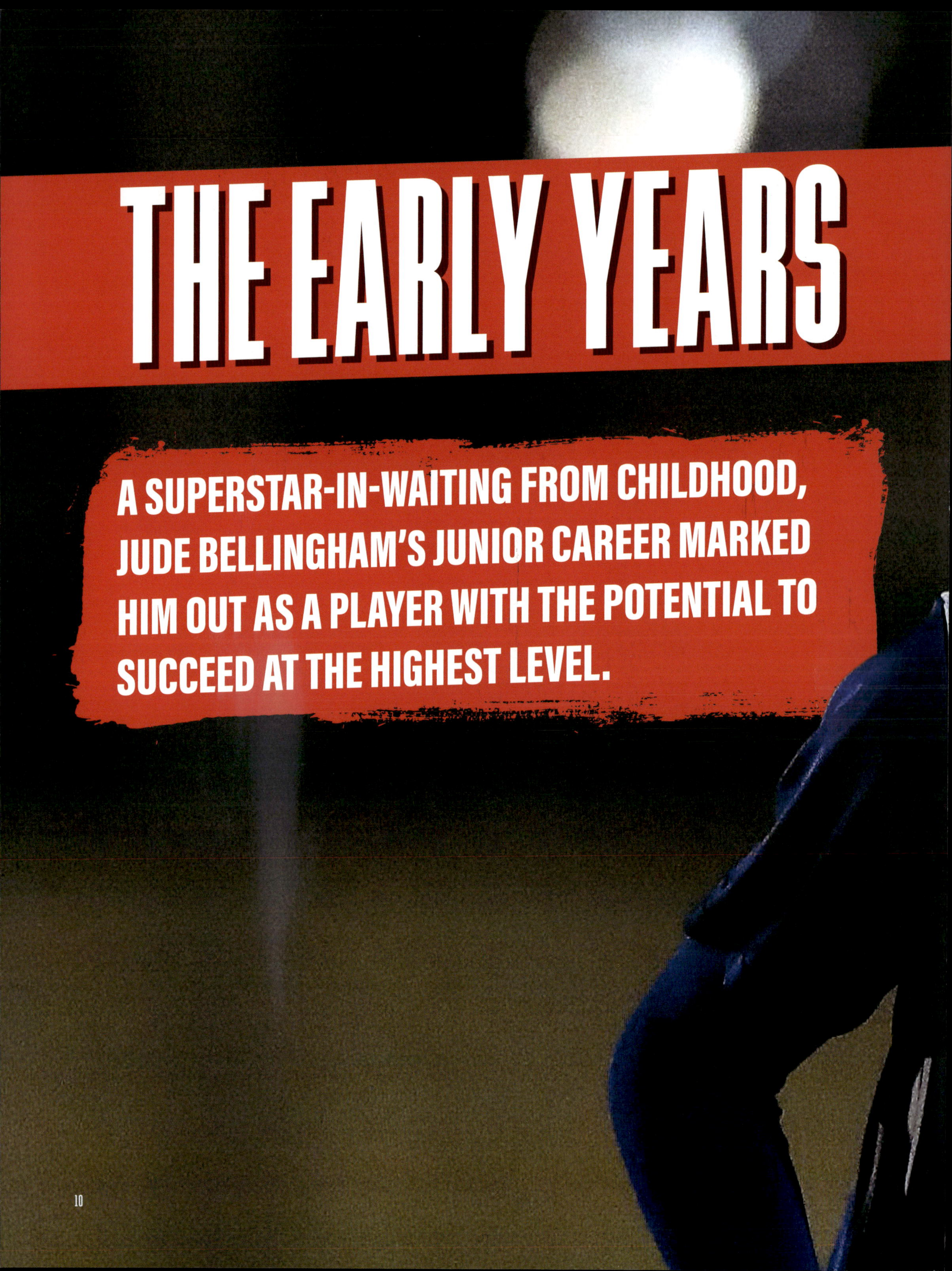

adidas
utilita
life with power

You would be forgiven if you thought Bellingham fell in love with the beautiful game from the first moment he kicked a football as a young boy in the West Midlands. A burning ambition to grow up and become a professional footballer is a familiar story told by many of the game's elite players but Bellingham's own remarkable journey, taking him with breathtaking speed from Birmingham City via Germany to Spain and the bright lights of Real Madrid, was not initially a typical one.

Born 15 miles from Birmingham in the small town of Stourbridge in the summer of 2003, Bellingham certainly grew up in a home with a footballing pedigree. His father Mark was a prolific striker in non-league football, as well as a sergeant with the West Midlands Police, scoring more than 700 goals in a semi-professional career that continued well beyond his 40th birthday. But despite watching his father torment opposition defences most weekends and being introduced to the game at an early age, Bellingham was not initially a convert.

"At first I didn't like football," he said. "I know it's incredible, because if someone took football away from me now, I would go crazy. I used to go to my first

"At first I didn't like football. I know it's incredible, because if someone took football away from me now, I would go crazy."

training sessions and pick grass and flowers. I used to make a small bouquet of daisies for my mother. My parents never pressured me. My father kept taking

OPPOSITE: **The Blues shaped Bellingham's career over a decade, identifying his talent from an early age.**

me, but he told me, if you want to play hide-and-seek or pick flowers, you can do that. My parents never forced me to do anything as long as I was a good boy and took care of others."

His early reluctance to get involved was noted by Phil Wooldridge, coach with Bellingham's first junior side Stourbridge Rovers. "As soon as you put a football in front of him, he was not really interested," he said. "It took a while for him to get into football. It wasn't just overnight. It was a matter of a few months."

When the youngster did eventually catch the football bug, however, there was no looking back. Bellingham now had a dream, telling his teachers

Bellingham now had a dream, telling his teachers and classmates that one day he would play for England.

and classmates that one day he would play for England, and as his career blossomed in those very early years, it was obvious he had the raw talent to potentially fulfil that dream. The next step in his development was a part-time move to the junior ranks of a professional club and with Birmingham, Wolves, West Bromwich Albion and Aston Villa all a short drive from the family home in Stourbridge, Bellingham's parents were not short of options.

It was The Blues who convinced the family that Bellingham's future lay at St Andrew's, although in truth the youngster did not need much persuading. "For Jude, there was never a doubt he would play for Birmingham City," his mother Denise said. "He went there as a seven-year-old and never wanted to leave." Bellingham by now may have been imagining

"It took a while for him to get into football."

his future as a footballer but for Denise sport was not yet the most important part of her son's life. "You don't send your child to football training with the plan that he'll one day turn professional," she said. "He was having fun, that was the most important thing."

His link-up with City saw Mark and Denise make the trip to the club's Academy HQ four times a week. The family eventually moved to Bromsgrove to be nearer to the training ground at Wast Hills while Birmingham enrolled Bellingham at the Priory School in Edgbaston. The young boy who had at first preferred flower arranging to football was now showing a growing and fierce dedication to his game and as he progressed impressively at Birmingham, it was clear Bellingham was one to watch.

"If he wasn't happy with a session, if he wasn't happy with the kind of route that his development in was going, he would be the first person to let me know his thoughts," Mike Dodds, one of his first

"He wasn't technically that far ahead of a lot of the boys, but he had a real appetite for the game."

coaches at Birmingham, told the BBC. "What made Jude stand out initially when he came in when he was seven or eight was just his general enthusiasm for football. He wasn't technically that far ahead of a lot of the boys, but he had a real appetite for the game. What made him different to other players that I've coached in the past is his desire to get better in every element of his game from a very early age. His general desire and application to be the best and be different was the thing that stood out."

RIGHT: Four years younger than many of his team-mates, Bellingham was a star for the Birmingham Under-18 side.

Although he was now being exposed regularly to a professional coaching set-up with City, the influence of his family remained as important as ever. "My family have always kept me grounded and given me a really good support network," he told the FA website in 2021. "I was actually a forward in my first few years at the Academy. After all, I had seen my dad score goals so often and always really enjoyed the atmosphere at non-league matches. When I was a young boy, I really wanted to be like him. But over the years I began to realise that I could make better use of my qualities in midfield.

"I had seen my dad score goals so often and always really enjoyed the atmosphere at non-league matches."

"We talk about footballing heroes, and my dad was my first. When you go and watch him play every week in non-league, you know it's not the Premier League or anything, but seeing the way he played and the atmosphere, it made me fall in love with football. Growing up, he'd always give me tips on what I could do and now it sort of flips and that's brilliant because we have that sort of relationship like father and son and then as I got older, like coach and player."

"My relationship with mom and dad is close and gives me balance. I received different things from my parents. They had jobs their entire lives before leading my career. Then I saw how they handled situations, especially since I turned professional. They do such a good job, with no real experience, and I always wonder how they do it. I admire how they could find themselves in any environment and be the best."

With his parents firmly behind him, Bellingham continued to make a name for himself in the Midlands.

"My family have always kept me grounded."

He played for the Blues Under-18 team at the age of 14 and made his debut for the club's Under-23 side in late 2018 when he was just 15.

He played for the Blues Under-18 team at the age of 14 and made his debut for the club's Under-23 side in late 2018 when he was just 15, scoring the only goal of the game against Nottingham Forest from the bench to underline his incredible potential. Already an England youth international, he was named one of the 50 most exciting teenagers in English football by *FourFourTwo* magazine in early 2019, describing him as "as a modern-day midfield schemer with lovely balance, tons of creativity and an eye for goal" and although he had not yet celebrated his 16th birthday, it had become only a matter of time before the youngster would chalk up his first major career milestone and play for the Birmingham first team.

BLUES BREAKTHROUGH

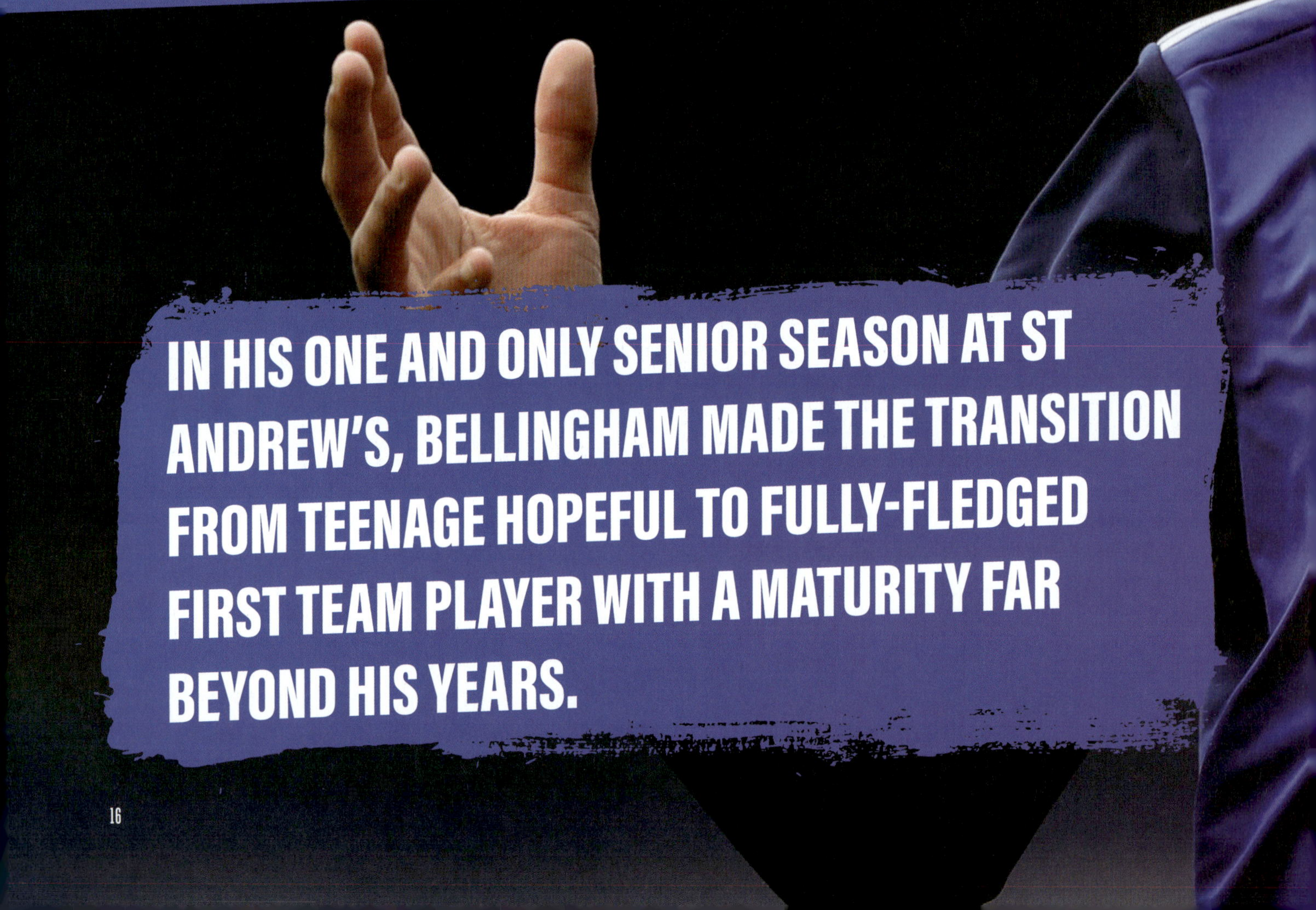

IN HIS ONE AND ONLY SENIOR SEASON AT ST ANDREW'S, BELLINGHAM MADE THE TRANSITION FROM TEENAGE HOPEFUL TO FULLY-FLEDGED FIRST TEAM PLAYER WITH A MATURITY FAR BEYOND HIS YEARS.

NHS
THANK YOU
BIRMINGHAM CITY
FOOTBALL CLUB
1875
BoyleSports
THIS IS BETTING.

There's a famous saying that preparation is the key to success and it was one which Birmingham followed to the letter as they carefully nurtured Bellingham's talent at the start of his career. By the time he was in his mid-teens, the club were already convinced he was destined for great things and it was merely a question of how they would manage his progress and gradually introduce the midfielder into their professional ranks.

The first step came in March 2019 when manager Garry Monk included Bellingham in his playing group for the Championship clash against West Brom at the Hawthorns. The youngster was the '19th man', not making the bench for the game, but warmed up with the team before kick-off to acclimatise him to the matchday experience. That summer, soon after he turned 16, he was handed a two-year scholarship deal and travelled with the senior professionals on the club's preseason training camp in Portugal. As the 2019-20 league season loomed, Bellingham was handed the No. 22 squad number and it was clear his senior bow was imminent.

"We put a plan in place where we were integrating him into first team training on an ad-hoc basis, then a

ABOVE: Bellingham's first team debut in 2019 against Portsmouth soon after celebrating his 16th birthday.

OPPOSITE: The teenager's first professional goal came against Stoke at St Andrew's.

LEFT: Bellingham signed for Birmingham in the summer of 2019.

Bellingham was handed the No. 22 squad number.

regular basis, then we had him part of the matchday squad as an observer, and then part of the matchday squad taking part in the warm-up," said Kristjaan Speakman, Birmingham's Academy manager. "We were well aware that at some point in the first half of this season, the player would make his debut. Whenever that happens there are inevitably a lot of eyes and a lot of pressure but we wanted to make that as seamless and as comfortable as possible. When you have the unique opportunity to follow a player like Jude's journey, it is an incredible thing for all of our staff that they have been able to see this boy grow and develop from a cheeky nine-year-old. He had always managed to cope with playing in a higher age group partly because he is such an intelligent player."

> *"He had always managed to cope with playing in a higher age group partly because he is such an intelligent player."*

The Blues had changed managers in the summer, with Spaniard Pep Clotet replacing Monk, but the revamped coaching set-up made no difference to Bellingham's trajectory and in early August 2019 he made his eagerly anticipated and record-breaking debut, starting in the League Cup clash with Portsmouth. Aged just 16 years and 38 days he became the youngest player in Birmingham's history, eclipsing the previous mark set by St Andrew's legend Trevor Francis back in 1970 by 101 days. The *Birmingham Mail* named the teenager the Man of the Match after his first senior appearance.

"We are aware he is being watched."

Less than three weeks later he got his first taste of Championship football, coming on as a 76th-minute substitute against Swansea, and he found the net for the first time in his career just six days later with the winner in the Blues' 2-1 victory against Stoke at St Andrew's. His goal set another notable record as Bellingham, now 16 years and 63 days old, wrote his name into the history books as the club's youngest ever scorer.

Outrageously early in his career, he was already a fixture in the first team. With each appearance under Clotet he improved and in December he was named the EFL Young Player of the Month. "The opportunity the head coach has given me to play has been amazing," he said after collecting the award. "I feel like every game I am growing and learning in a great league where you need to show you can handle men's football. Now I really want to kick on and see what I can achieve."

The quality of the 16-year-old's displays however were a mixed blessing for the Blues. His impact was sensational but his burgeoning reputation meant he was now on the radar of rival clubs in England and further afield. "We are aware he is being watched," admitted Clotet. "He has been watched since he was 13 or 14. For the Middlesbrough game [in late January] half of Europe was here. The more games that he has played, the more difficult it has become for me to see a ceiling on his performances. We started him in a position that would suit him and release some of the pressure on him, as a kind of false winger. Slowly we moved him into the midfield where he could gain more confidence. Now we are playing him in his position in a more advanced role. It took some careful planning to make sure that he would make it."

It was not only scouts from big clubs who began to take a keen interest in the teenager. "Bellingham is more than a potion of potential because he is performing now," wrote Ben Fisher in *The Guardian* in February. "Those who work with Bellingham highlight his bite, work ethic and notably the physical strides he has made over the past months. His manager revealed Bellingham had grown 2.4cm since the start of the season and there is a sense he will end up as a No. 8, though he has thrived on both flanks."

"Those who work with Bellingham highlight his bite, work ethic and notably the physical strides he has made over the past months."

The remainder of the season saw Birmingham embroiled in a dogfight to avoid relegation but Bellingham was unfazed by the intensity of the situation and as the summer transfer window

LEFT: Spanish manager Pep Coltet was the man who gave the young midfielder his first taste of first team football.

His 44th and final game for City came in July against Derby County.

approached, the rumour mill refused to be silenced. Premier League heavyweights Manchester United, Liverpool, Chelsea and Arsenal were all linked with the player while Real Madrid, Barcelona, Bayern Munich and Borussia Dortmund led the European contingent of interested clubs. In the end it became a two-horse race between United and Dortmund for the youngster's signature. Both offered Birmingham an initial transfer fee of £25 million for Bellingham and in July the Blues, under financial pressure to balance the books, reluctantly agreed to sell to the German club.

His 44th and final game for City came in July against Derby County, just two days after passing his medical at Dortmund. It was an emotional afternoon at St Andrew's after his breakthrough season and after the final whistle, a tearful Bellingham and his family said their goodbyes to the Blues faithful from the pitch. "We've shed a few tears," he said. "I tried my best to hide it but sometimes it's difficult. I am a massive fan of the club. I fell in love with Birmingham City and then fell in love with football. So just to get a little bit of time out there on my own and with my little brother, mum and dad meant the world to us."

The teenager's time in England's second city may have been brief but it was long enough nonetheless for the midfielder to leave a legacy. Voted the City Young Player of the Year and the EFL Young Player of the Season, he was also named the Championship Apprentice Player of the Year. More importantly, he helped ensure Birmingham avoided relegation and in recognition of his contribution, the club announced they were retiring his already iconic No. 22 shirt after his departure.

ABOVE: Bellingham's brief Birmingham career came to an end in July 2020 in front of the City fans.

RECORD-BREAKING WONDERKID

From the moment he made his senior debut for Birmingham City while still studying for his GCSEs, Bellingham has been reinventing ideas about what age a young player can achieve at the highest level.

In the early stages of his career, Bellingham seemed to set a new record with almost every appearance. His bow for Birmingham in August 2019, becoming the youngest player ever to represent the club only 38 days after turning 16, was only the first of many career milestones. Wayne Rooney, another of England's most famous teenage talents, was nine months older than Bellingham when he got his first taste of first team action for Everton back in 2002.

After his move to Germany and Borussia Dortmund in the summer of 2020, Bellingham relentlessly continued to rewrite the record books. The Bundesliga club's youngest goal scorer, the teenager also became the youngest Dortmund captain in history in October 2022. In the same month he featured in the Champions League against Lazio at the age of 17 years and 113 days, the youngest English footballer to play in Europe's top tier club competition. England team-mate Phil Foden had previously held the record after playing for Manchester City against Feyenoord in late 2017.

ABOVE: Bellingham's exploits have seen him eclipse many of the game's young guns.

OPPOSITE TOP: Theo Walcott is the youngest footballer ever to play for England.

OPPOSITE BELOW: Man City's Phil Foden previously held the record as the youngest Englishman to feature in the Champions League.

The midfielder made a total of 92 appearances in the Bundesliga. No other teenager has played as many games in the German top division.

At international level Bellingham has to concede the record as the youngest Three Lion. He was 17 years and 136 days old when he came off the bench against the Republic of Ireland in 2020 but winger Theo Walcott was younger when he won his first cap against Hungary 14 years earlier. Bellingham was also 25 days older than Rooney when he made his England bow in 2003. Michael Owen, another teenager who had burst onto the international scene at an early age, had already celebrated his 18th birthday by the time he was capped.

The Real Madrid star is however the leader of the pack in terms of current England players. Of the squad that went so close at Euro 2024, defender Luke Shaw was the next youngest debutant for the Three Lions. He was 18 years, seven months and 21 days when he played against Denmark in 2014 while midfielder Kobbie Mainoo was 27 days short of his 19th birthday when he came on as a replacement against Brazil in a friendly three months before the Euros.

Bukayo Saka was also 19 when he started his England career while Phil Foden was in his 20s when he first pulled on the famous white shirt for a senior fixture.

When Gareth Southgate selected Bellingham for Euro 2020, the 17-year-old joined an exclusive club of England players to be picked for the World Cup or European Championships while still teenagers. Only 11 players had achieved the feat before him while Saka also set the same milestone when he was named in the same squad. The youngest in this category was again Walcott, who was only 17 years and 85 days old when he included in Sven-Göran Eriksson's squad for the 2006 World Cup but did not play a single minute in Germany as England reached the last eight of the tournament.

BUNDESLIGA STAR

A SERIAL RECORD BREAKER IN GERMANY, BELLINGHAM BLOSSOMED ON FOREIGN FIELDS TO ESTABLISH HIMSELF AS ONE OF EUROPEAN FOOTBALL'S BRIGHTEST AND MOST COVETED TALENTS.

BVB
DORTMUND
22
BELLINGHAM

> **"Unlike their competitors, Dortmund offer that most precious of commodities – guaranteed game time."**

"I am incredibly excited to have joined one of Europe's biggest clubs," Bellingham said after meeting his new Borussia Dortmund team-mates for the first time in preseason in the summer of 2020, just eight days after his final game for Birmingham. "The direction they are heading in and how much they help to improve young players made it an easy decision for myself and my family. This is the best place for me to carry on my development."

His decision to sign for BVB, as the club is commonly known in Germany, rather than Manchester United and the chance to play in the Premier League surprised some but others argued it was the smart move for the teenager. "Unlike their competitors, Dortmund offer that most precious of commodities – guaranteed game time," the *Sky Sports* website said. "They do not offer 10 to 12 league games a season and a place on the bench in the Champions League. They offer 30 league games and a starting XI shirt in Europe. In terms of time on the pitch, the likes of Barcelona and Real Madrid simply cannot compete. Dortmund are not recruiting academy prospects, they are recruited as first-team players."

The deal to take Bellingham to the Bundesliga made him the most expensive 17-year-old player in the history of football but he was to prove unfazed by the record price tag or the dramatic increase in his wages from £145 per week as an apprentice to a reported £50,000 per week. His mother Denise relocated to Germany to ensure her son was not overawed by his new surroundings, leaving his father Mark back home with his younger brother Jobe, and

> **The deal to take Bellingham to the Bundesliga made him the most expensive 17-year-old player in the history of football.**

Progress at club level continued to be meteoric.

OPPOSITE: The midfielder signed for Dortmund hoping to take his club career to the next level.

BELOW: Bellingham enjoyed a dream, goalscoring debut for his new team in 2020.

the Dortmund faithful waited expectantly to see what the teenager who had only played second-tier football in England was really capable of.

Before his debut however Bellingham had to select his shirt number and he again opted for 22, the same number he had worn on his back with obvious pride at St Andrew's. "There's an actual reason for the number," Bellingham explained. "The manager wanted to send a message to me that my position on the pitch could not be pinned down easily. For him, I wasn't a number 10, an eight or a four but all of them together. Which adds up to 22."

His three seasons with Dortmund were nothing short of sensational. Bellingham's first appearance came in the German Cup against Duisburg in September and he sent out an immediate message with a goal on debut in a 5-0 triumph. At 17 years, two months and 16 days, he became the competition's youngest ever scorer. Five days later he made his Bundesliga bow against Borussia Mönchengladbach and set up fellow teenager Gio Reyna for the second score in a 3-0 win. Once again it was history in the making as Bellingham and Reyna, with a total age of only 34, became the Bundesliga's youngest ever pairing to combine for a goal.

Capped by England at senior level for the first time in October, Bellingham's progress at club level continued to be meteoric. He opened his Bundesliga account in April against Stuttgart and later the same month was on target for the first time in the Champions League against Manchester City at the Westfalenstadion, the youngest player ever to net for BVB in European club football's marquee tournament.

ABOVE: Bellingham teamed up with fellow Englishman Jadon Sancho in Germany.

RIGHT: Bellingham was a German Cup winner in only his first season with Dortmund.

The undisputed highlight of the season however came in May as Dortmund thrashed RB Leipzig 4-1 in Berlin in the final of the German Cup.

The undisputed highlight of the season however came in May as Dortmund thrashed RB Leipzig 4-1 in Berlin in the final of the German Cup, giving Bellingham the first winner's medal of his short career and BVB the club's first major silverware in four years.

Between 2021 and 2023, the young midfielder's incredible progression in the game only accelerated. In late 2021 he was nominated for the prestigious Golden Boy award, presented to best player under 21 in Europe, and later the same month he scored an unforgettable solo goal for BVB against Bielefeld, sublimely beating three defenders in the box before chipping the goalkeeper with his weaker left foot.

His final season in Germany, the 2022-23 campaign, was his finest. In September he became the youngest player, aged 19 and 80 days, to make a century of appearances for Dortmund, the milestone fittingly coming in the traditional Ruhr derby against Schalke. A few weeks later he was handed the captain's armband for the first time against Cologne, making him BVB's youngster ever skipper. "When I first signed for this club, it's something that I never even thought was possible until I met the players and realised that they can give me the belief to one day be the captain," he said. "It's something that other people always mentioned to me and I brushed off. I am really grateful to be given the chance today."

Dortmund agonisingly missed out on the Bundesliga title to Bayern Munich on the last day of the domestic campaign but on an individual level, it had been an outstanding year for Bellingham. No Dortmund player made more appearances (42) in all competitions than the young Englishman and he top scored for BVB with 14 goals. His stylish and endlessly energetic efforts in Borussia's engine room earned him the *ESPN* Midfielder of the Year award and a place in the Bundesliga Team of the Year.

More significantly, in May he was voted the Bundesliga Player of the Year. "His talent has been obvious for all to see ever since making the switch to Germany from Birmingham City in 2019," reported the official Bundesliga website. "Although he has gone from strength to strength with each passing campaign, he has blossomed into arguably his team's most influential player this time around. In some matches, the teenager has been simply unplayable There's no doubt that the teenager – and yes, he is still only 19 until the end of June 2023 – is destined for greatness in the footballing world.

"It is no exaggeration to say this season that Bellingham has shown flashes of the characteristics of some iconic players; the grace of a forward moving Zinedine Zidane, for example, or the tough tackling and determination of a Steven Gerrard or Patrick Vieira. Like those aforementioned legends, Bellingham is also unafraid to voice his opinion to team-mates almost twice his age and has since remoulded that burning desire for those around him to follow his never-say-die attitude into a force for positive encouragement."

It was high praise indeed but little did German football fans realise at the time that the kind words would be the epitaph to his brilliant three-year stint in their country. Only weeks later it was announced the star would be a Real Madrid player the following season and for the second time in his career, Bellingham said goodbye as he embarked on a new, even greater challenge.

"It was funny because he was quite shy and quiet."

Dortmund Team-mates

Signing for BVB from Birmingham City, Bellingham now found himself lining up alongside a host of exciting world-class players in Germany.

The arrival of the 17-year-old midfielder at Signal Iduna Park was the second time in the space of three seasons Dortmund had welcomed one of English football's brightest young talents. The club had signed compatriot Jadon Sancho in 2017 from the Manchester City Academy at the same age and as the senior member of what was a youthful England duo, Sancho helped Bellingham adapt during his debut season.

They played 35 times together in 2021-22, winning the German Cup final, before Sancho left for Manchester United but not before the two England stars had forged a close bond both on and off the pitch.

"He is a great footballer, he is mature for his age."

OPPOSITE: The England star spent two seasons with Erling Haaland before the striker signed for Manchester City.

BELOW: Bellingham learnt much from Dortmund skipper Marco Reus during his Bundesliga career.

"The sky's the limit for the guy," Sancho said in 2021. "He is a great footballer, he is mature for his age, which is very surprising. I think when I was a teenager, I was not that mature at all. The sky's the limit for him and if he keeps on doing well, he can reach the top of his ability."

The former team-mates found themselves on opposing sides in 2024 the Champions League final at Wembley which they both started, Bellingham as a Real Madrid player while Sancho was back at BVB on loan from Old Trafford. "I remember when he came to Dortmund," Sancho said before the game. "It was funny because he was quite shy and quiet. Now we are really close. Every time I see him, I check up on him and see how he's doing."

Striker Erling Haaland scored 70 goals for Dortmund in the two years he spent in the side while Bellingham pulled the strings in midfield before the Norwegian left the club for England and Manchester City. The forward had a front row seat to witness some of Bellingham's achievements – they played 65 games together – and was on the pitch with him in Turkey in late 2021 when BVB beat Besiktas 2-1 in the Champions League.

Bellingham scored the first and set-up Haaland for the second in Istanbul. His brilliant performance saw the midfielder become the youngest player ever to score in back-to-back Champions League appearances, as well as the youngest England player to net away from home in the history of the competition. "Jude is amazing," Haaland said in his post-match interview. "He's only 18, three years younger than me, and plays so incredibly well. It's crazy. What can I say? He's amazing."

The Dortmund captain when Bellingham joined, Marco Reus played over 400 games for the club and scored 170 goals. A regular for Germany for a decade, the forward was struck immediately by the teenager's maturity and potential.

"From day one, he has not shied away from taking responsibility in midfield," he told *The Guardian* in 2022. "He never seemed to be intimidated by playing against 25-year-olds or really experienced players. I must admit I didn't know too much about him when he came. But my first impression was that he already had something to his game in all aspects of his position that I had never seen before for a player of his age. At 19, he's taking steps towards reaching his full potential, which will make him one of the very best players in the game."

Dortmund Managers

"With someone like him, I don't look at the date of birth."

Three different coaches helped Bellingham forge his reputation as one of the game's hottest talents during his three years in Germany.

Swiss coach Lucien Favre had been in the dugout at the Westfalenstadion for two seasons when Bellingham signed for the Black and Yellows. A two-time league title winner as manager in his native Switzerland with FC Zurich, he was the man charged with carefully developing the young midfielder in his new, unfamiliar surroundings and it did not take the teenager long to impress.

"With someone like him, I don't look at the date of birth," Favre said shortly after the transfer was completed, referencing his obvious first team inexperience. "It's easy for me to work with such a talent. He's great young guy in every single way. I like his mentality, the willingness to work for the team, the intensity with which he plays football, the will to win and the solutions he finds on the football pitch.

"First and foremost, I am interested in playing intelligence. He has the technical skills and a feel for space. During pre-season, I've already got to know

"We don't even know how good he is yet."

him better. I like the way he handles the ball, how he defends it. Jude gives us many tactical possibilities and has an amazing presence. He can play as a number six or number eight, is a good passer, and tries to put himself in a finishing position. With him, many different systems are possible."

Less than six months after signing, Favre was sacked and replaced on an interim basis by Edin Terzić. The German steered the ship for the remainder of the 2020-21 campaign, winning the German Cup, and returned as manager on a full-time basis in the summer of 2022.

"We don't even know how good he is yet," he said during his second spell in charge, Bellingham's third and final season with BVB. "We're trying to figure out where his limit is going to be. Borussia Dortmund is known for offering young talents the platform to play at the highest level. I think he's the oldest 19-year-old I've ever seen. Not only do we benefit from him but the club is also the right step for him. Jude will have a big impact not only with us but also with the England national team. We want to support him in pushing his limits further."

In between Terzic's two stints on the touchline, fellow German Marco Rose was the Dortmund manager for the 2021-22 season. Three months into his reign Bellingham scored arguably the best goal of his BVB career, a stunning solo effort against Bielefeld in the Bundesliga.

"Jude's an outstanding lad," he said after the game. "He's been an ever-present for weeks now. He's in a great frame of mind and gives us so much. He never stops running and just plays so well. I love the way he plays football. He is an aggressive player who does so much for the team but also plays football with such confidence for his relative young age. His movement is always very good."

It was a brief working relationship between player and manager but the close bond they formed was illustrated in 2024 when they were reunited when Real Madrid played Rose's RB Leipzig, his hometown club, at the Bernabéu in the Last 16 of the Champions League. Los Blancos knocked out the Germans but the enduring image of the night was Bellingham and Rose in a long and heartfelt hug on the pitch after the final whistle.

OPPOSITE: Lucien Favre found a willing pupil in Bellingham.

BELOW: Edin Terzić nurtured Bellingham during his two spells at BVB.

Bellingham quickly adapted to the pace and style of the Bundesliga.

In total, Bellingham scored 24 times for the Germans between 2020 and 2023.

Celebrating after scoring against Besiktas in September 2021, one of his eight Champions League goals for Dortmund.

THE COMPLETE PACKAGE

Blessed with natural pace, power and poise, Bellingham's skill set and natural physique make him one of the most dynamic players on the planet.

Of all the positions on the pitch, the role of the modern midfielder is by a distance the most technically and physically demanding. Charged with creating and scoring at one end and disrupting the opposition at the other, as well as tirelessly covering the space between the two, elite midfielders are both workhorses and artists and few have all the attributes to fulfil every aspect of the role. Bellingham ticks every box.

In possession he is superb and since his senior debut for Birmingham in 2019, he has an average passing accuracy of over 90 per cent. He rarely surrenders the ball and his reliable distribution and trademark lay-offs make him a natural focal point. His ability to dribble, an increasingly rare quality in the modern game, adds a crucial unpredictable element to his play and is a trait which opposition managers cannot plan to contain in the middle of the park.

ABOVE: **Bellingham had to learn quickly after he was thrust into the Birmingham team as a 16-year-old.**

OPPOSITE: **The international learned to play in a number of different positions during his three seasons in Germany.**

Bellingham's tackling is strong. In La Liga in 2023-24, he won 81% of his challenges (and over 93% at the 2022 World Cup with England in Qatar) while in his first year in Spain, he came out on top in more than half of his one-on-one duels with 188 successful challenges. At six foot one tall, he is a significant presence in the air and in the 2023-24 Champions League won over 60% of his aerial duels, as well as making seven interceptions and five penalty area clearances in Europe.

Discipline is a key part of the midfielder's role and despite his still relative inexperience, the young Englishman has an impressive record. He has averaged only one yellow card in every five appearances in his career so far and has been sent off just once in more than in nearly 250 games for Birmingham, Dortmund, Madrid and England.

His versatility is one of his greatest assets. First played on the left at St Andrew's before moving more centrally later in the season, he was a traditional central midfielder for much of his time in Germany but as his career has progressed, Bellingham has played across every position in the middle and was deployed to devastating effect at the Bernabéu in a more advanced role, leading to his prolific 23-goal haul in Spain.

Unsurprisingly his shot accuracy for Los Blancos was high, with over 71% of his attempts on goal on target. His rate of 0.74 goals per game placed him in the top one per cent of players in the division while his 0.97 goal contributions for every appearance also saw him rated at the top of the overall creativity charts.

Naturally right-footed, 27 of his 51 club goals between 2019 and 2024 came from his stronger side but he has underlined his all-round game with 11 with his left, as well as six headed goals amongst his growing tally.

At 21, Bellingham's development is still a work in progress despite his achievements. However, there is already no doubt the precious raw ingredients, the blistering acceleration, the eye for goal and the fighting spirit, are all in place.

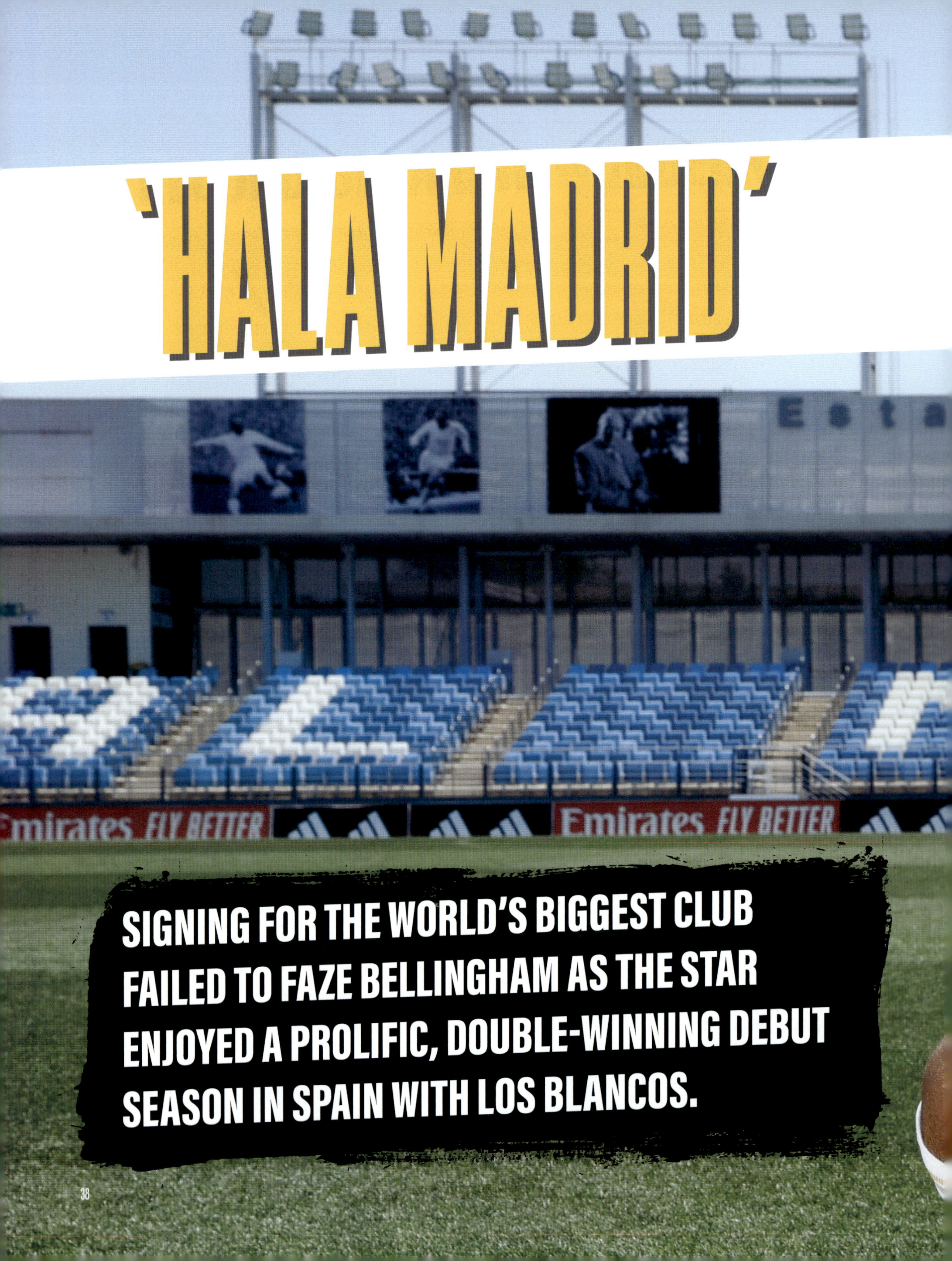

'HALA MADRID'

SIGNING FOR THE WORLD'S BIGGEST CLUB FAILED TO FAZE BELLINGHAM AS THE STAR ENJOYED A PROLIFIC, DOUBLE-WINNING DEBUT SEASON IN SPAIN WITH LOS BLANCOS.

FIFA
WORLD CHAMPIONS
2022
14
UEFA
FOUNDATION
for children
15 de junio de 2023
Emirates
FLY BETTER
es FLY BETTER

When Real Madrid completed the transfer of Bellingham to the Bernabéu in June 2023, the player was still 15 days shy of celebrating his 20th birthday. The fee of £88.5 million, potentially rising to £115 million, the Spanish giants invested on the six-year deal they handed to the youngster made him the club's second biggest signing of all time, second only to Eden Hazard's move from Chelsea four years earlier. It also made him the third most expensive teenager in the history of the world game after Kylian Mbappé and João Félix.

The sixth Englishman and seventh British player to join Los Blancos in the club's professional era, he was the first to arrive from a Continental club rather than directly from an English side. Bellingham's age was brought into sharp focus by the realisation he had been born in 2003 just three days before Madrid had unveiled David Beckham.

"This is the proudest day of my life, the day when I join the greatest football club in the history of the game," Bellingham said. "I want to thank, most importantly, my family for all the support and making the deal as easy as possible. I don't think about money at all when I make these kinds of decisions. I never have, I never will. I loved the feeling I got from the club, I couldn't hide it. I told them more or less straight away how I felt."

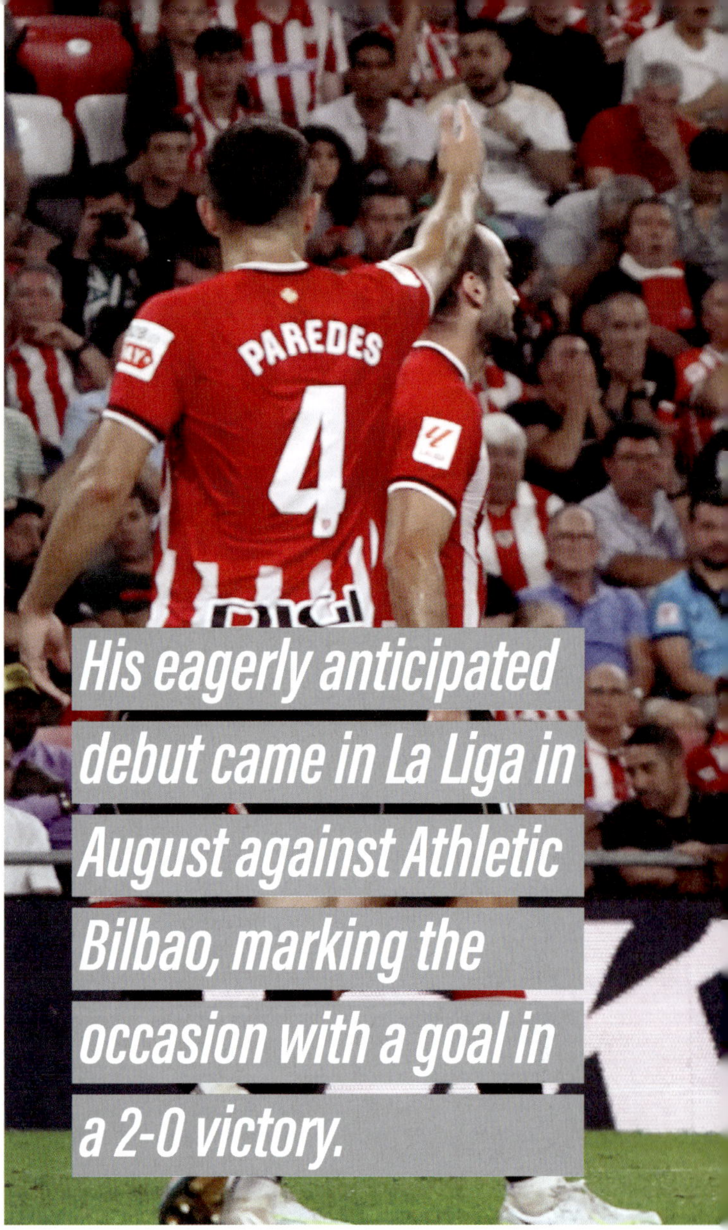

His eagerly anticipated debut came in La Liga in August against Athletic Bilbao, marking the occasion with a goal in a 2-0 victory.

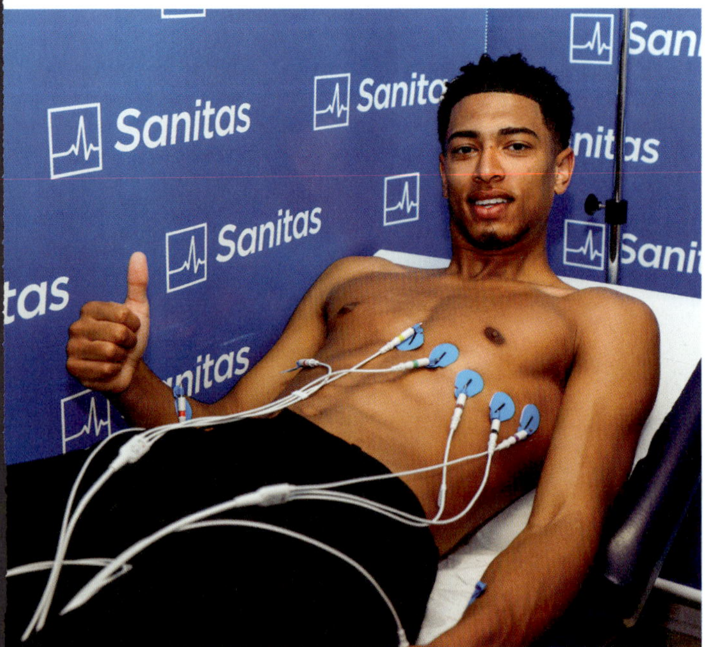

There were of course doubts that Bellingham might struggle with the global profile that inevitably comes with playing for Los Blancos, the 14-time European champions, his hefty price tag and or even the fact he was handed the iconic Madrid No. 5 shirt, famously worn by his legendary childhood hero Zinedine

Zidane, but they were all were comprehensively dispelled from day one in Spain.

His eagerly anticipated debut came in La Liga in August against Athletic Bilbao, marking the occasion with a goal in a 2-0 victory. Deployed by manager Carlo Ancelotti in a more advanced, attacking role, he was on target in his next two appearances for the club but all three matches had been away from home and it was not until early September that the Bernabéu faithful had the chance to see their exciting new signing in the flesh. Bellingham did not disappoint, scoring a dramatic injury-time winner against Getafe, sparking ecstatic scenes in

ABOVE: Bellingham marked his debut for Los Blancos with a goal against Athletic Bilbao.

OPPOSITE: The star passed his Madrid medical in the summer of 2023 ahead of his record-breaking transfer.

the capacity 85,000-strong crowd. For the first but not the last time in the Spanish capital, Bellingham responded with his trademark goal celebration, stretching out both arms horizontally in a joyous acknowledgement to his new fans.

The individual accolades for his superb start soon followed. Bellingham was named the Madrid Player of the Month for August, September and October

and he was voted La Liga Player of the Month in both August and October. When he scored twice in a 4-0 demolition of Osasuna in early October, his double took his tally to 10 goals in his first 10 appearances for Los Blancos, equalling the record for the best start in front of goal for a new Madrid player set by Cristiano Ronaldo in 2009. He netted his 14th goal of the campaign against Cádiz in November, surpassing the Portuguese great's previous club record of 13 in his opening 15 games. "I'm a confident guy but I didn't expect such a good start," Bellingham admitted. "At this stage of the season you can't ask for more."

Before the end of 2023 he had also picked up the Kopa Trophy and Golden Boy Award, both prestigious prizes presented to the best Under-21 player in the world and Europe respectively. Bellingham was the first Englishman to claim the Kopa Trophy.

If by now Bellingham was already a firm favourite with Los Blancos faithful, he elevated himself to undisputed hero status with his match-winning performances in the two La Liga clashes with Barcelona. 'El Clasico' is the most significant and intense game of any season for both of the Spanish giants and arguably the biggest club fixture on the planet and when Madrid needed him, Bellingham rose to the challenge. Losing 1-0 in the second half at the Nou Camp in October, the star scored with a stunning leveller from 30 yards out and in the 92nd minute volleyed home the winner to complete a sensational comeback and a fairy-tale El Clasico debut. In April at the Bernabéu he was the Madrid saviour once again, smashing in another second-half, injury-time winner to seal a 3-2 victory and propel Los Blancos closer to the title with only six league games remaining. His goal was his 21st for the club, earning him the distinction as the top-scoring Englishman in Real's history ahead of Beckham and Laurie Cunningham, who had played for the club in the 1980s.

With the league title in their sights courtesy of Bellingham's pivotal goals, Madrid made no mistake in those final six domestic fixtures. Four wins and two draws, in which the midfielder scored twice, were more than enough to secure the club's record-

ABOVE: The new signing was an immediate hit with the Madrid fans in Spain.

LEFT: Bellingham lifted the coveted Kopa Trophy, awarded to the world's best Under-21 player, in 2023.

OPPOSITE: Bellingham's goals against arch-rivals Barcelona ensured he became a firm favourite with the Bernabéu faithful.

'El Clasico' is the most significant and intense game.

extending 36th La Liga crown, finishing a comfortable 10 points clear of rivals Barcelona. For the first time in his career, Bellingham was now the proud owner of a league winner's medal.

"His debut campaign in Spain has been spectacularly successful," said *BBC Sport's* Andy West. "And it's

"His debut campaign in Spain has been spectacularly successful."

not just about his 18 league goals. The England midfielder's willingness to work tirelessly from box to box and his ability to create chances for team-mates have endeared him to the Bernabéu faithful. His stature as one of the best players in the world has clearly been enhanced."

Los Blancos' dominant domestic form – they lost just once in their 38 La Liga matches – was mirrored by their irresistible efforts in the Champions League and Bellingham was to the fore on European football's highest profile stage. He scored the winner on his competition debut for Madrid against Union Berlin

Bellingham was to the fore on European football's highest profile stage.

at the Bernabéu in September and was on target three more times as the side topped their group and cruised into the knockout stages.

There was drama throughout the business end of the tournament, not least in the second leg of the quarter-final clash with Manchester City. A 1-1 draw at the Etihad saw the tie go to a dreaded penalty shootout but Bellingham showed his nerve to coolly convert and Los Blancos emerged from an epic encounter as 4-3 winners from the spot. It was equally tense in the last four against Bayern Munich, with Madrid dramatically going through 4-3 on aggregate.

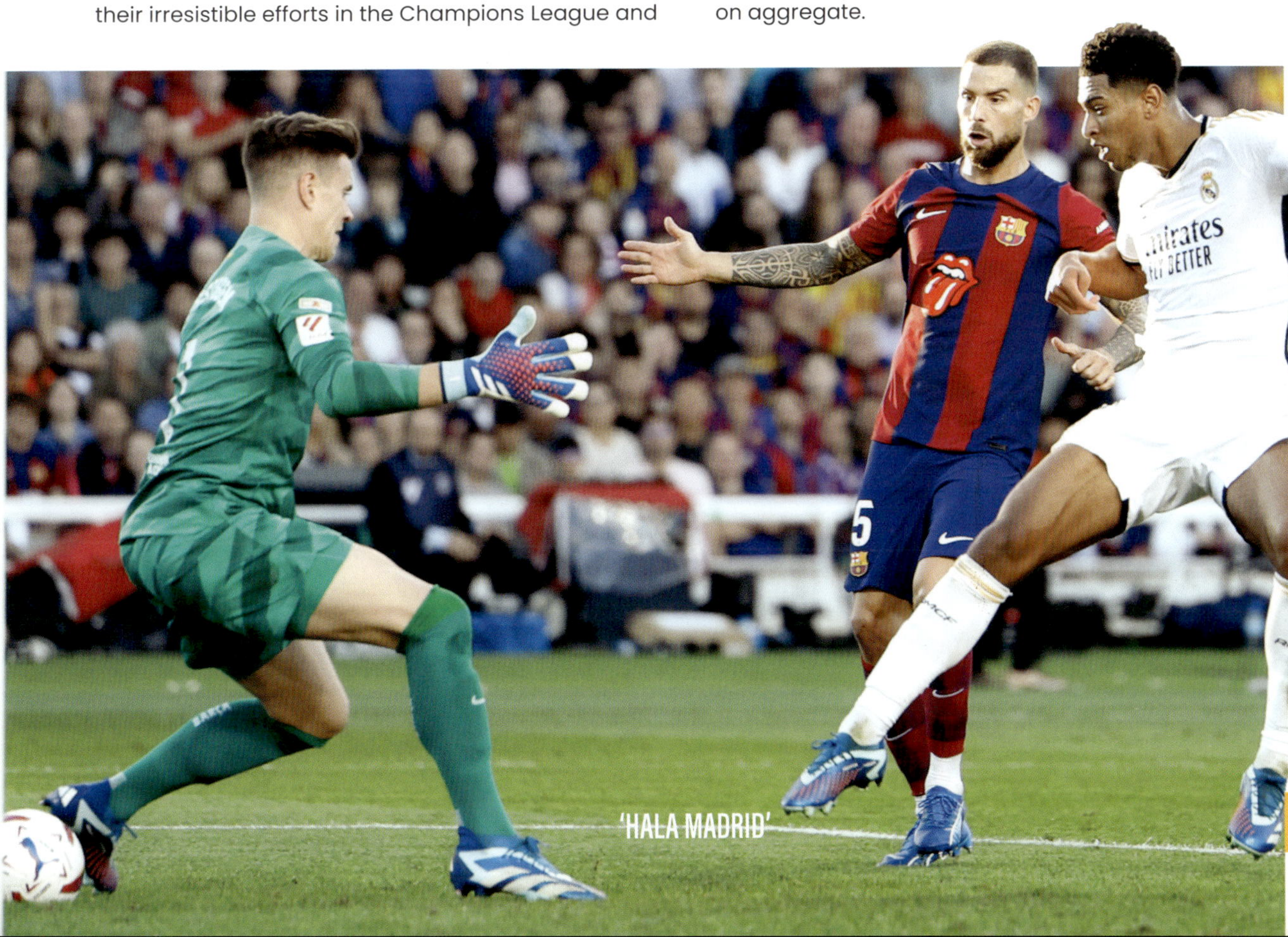

The footballing gods had decided it was Borussia Dortmund, Bellingham's former club, who stood between Madrid and an unprecedented 15th

After the final whistle, Bellingham went over to his mother Denise and placed his winner's medal over her neck.

European crown. The final at Wembley took the 20-year-old back home to England for his first Champions League final and the chance to cap a sensational first season with another major trophy.

Surrounded in the Madrid ranks by multiple Champions League winners, Bellingham betrayed no signs of his inexperience in London. Los Blancos

ABOVE: A European champion, the midfielder was appearing in his first Champions League final.

RIGHT: The whole Bellingham family were at Wembley to witness his night of European glory.

"I've always dreamed of playing in these games."

weathered BVB's first-half storm and in the second period Dani Carvajal gave the Spaniards the lead before Bellingham provided the inch-perfect pass in the 83rd minute that saw Vinicius Junior add the second. Madrid were the kings of Europe yet again and the new boy's dream debut season had just got even better. After the final whistle, Bellingham went over to his mother Denise and placed his winner's medal over her neck. She responded by kissing her son before she, his father Mark and brother Jobe joined him on the Wembley pitch to savour the moment.

"I've always dreamed of playing in these games," he said. "When it gets hard at times you start wonder if it's all worth it but nights like tonight make it all worth it. It's got to be up there in terms of the perfect season. It's the best night of my life. The club I'm now at is so special to me and so is my old club. It wouldn't be possible without Dortmund. I'll always be grateful and always have respect for what the club did for me."

As the dust settled on what Bellingham had achieved in his 10 short months in Spain, it was almost impossible to overstate his incredible and instant impact. His haul of 23 goals in 42 appearances in all competitions, the most prolific season of his career, was second only to Vinicius Junior and he was the club's leading marksman in La Liga with 19 in 28 games, as well as six assists. In the week leading up to the Champions League final his dazzling displays were rewarded when he was voted La Liga Player of the Season, receiving an award previously won by Spanish football greats Lionel Messi and Karim Benzema.

"I would like to dedicate it to my team-mates, the coaching staff and, most importantly, to the fans of

> *"It's a pleasure every time I play for this team. Hala Madrid."*

the best club in the world," he said. "It's a pleasure every time I play for this team. Hala Madrid."

There was one more individual accolade for Bellingham to enjoy during the 2023-24 season. It came in his new hometown in late April when he was handed the prestigious Laureus World Sports Breakthrough of the Year trophy. Bellingham rubbed shoulders with the likes of tennis superstar Novak Djokovic and Olympic legend Simone Biles at the glittering awards ceremony but his meteoric rise in Madrid was really brought home when Usain Bolt took to the stage and copied Bellingham's outstretched-arm celebration rather than reproducing his own, world-famous 'Lightning Bolt'. If any further proof were needed, it confirmed Bellingham was now a bona fide global sporting phenomenon in his own right.

"His appetite for the biggest games has been the defining feature of a stunning campaign," wrote Nick Wright for *Sky Sports*. "Bellingham had to step up, thrust into an advanced midfield role somewhere between a false nine and a number 10. It was new to him. It didn't show. Bellingham had demonstrated his scoring potential at Dortmund but this season has been something else. He surpassed his total of 14 goals last season in the space of only a few months. Madrid have been rewarded for putting him in better positions. Bellingham represents the club's present and future."

Bernabéu Team-mates

Surrounded by established superstars when he touched down in Spain, Bellingham wasted no time in joining the exclusive club with his remarkable, recording-breaking debut season in the capital.

Any player signing for Real Madrid, let alone a teenager who had never before played in La Liga, would be forgiven for feeling intimidated. The club's illustrious history, reputation and worldwide fame demand only football's finest pull on the iconic white shirt and when Bellingham reported for training for the first time in 2023, the assembled players were akin to a who's who of modern greats boasting an incredible, collective haul of major trophies.

It was not only the current squad that could have unsettled the young midfielder. The many legends to have graced the Bernabéu in the past, not least

"He is incredible and he always makes a difference."

OPPOSITE: Bellingham and Brazilian Vinicius Jr have forged a deadly partnership at the Bernabéu.

BELOW: The Englishman is part of the new generation of player to replace Madrid legends like Toni Kroos.

his own childhood hero Zinedine Zidane, cast an unforgiving shadow over the stadium but not for the first time in his career, Bellingham was undaunted. His impact in Madrid was instant and his team-mates were immediately won over by their English new boy.

"Our supporters got used to Cristiano Ronaldo, now Jude has arrived for us," said Brazilian forward Vinicius Junior, a worthy rival with Bellingham for the coveted 2024 Ballon d'Or and a Madrid player since 2018. "He is incredible and he always makes a difference. We are a lot of young players, we are always together on and off the field. This creates unity and makes us a good team that wants to improve and win a lot of things. He was born to play for Real Madrid and to define an era in the greatest team in the world. I hope this connection that we have lasts for the many years that we can play together. I love playing with Jude."

Bellingham was brought to Madrid to refresh Los Blancos' midfield and Toni Kroos, who enjoyed a trophy-laden decade at the Bernabéu before retiring at the end of 2023-24, was in no doubt about the quality of his heir apparent.

"He is already an absolute asset to the team," the 2014 World Cup winner with Germany said. "He's integrated surprisingly well in such a short space of time. I have a very good feeling about him because I believe he's incredibly mature, very advanced for his age, and not just mentally. The way he plays football is always clear in his actions and he plays to his strengths to the full. A lot of other people at that age still makes a lot of silly mistakes, either technical or tactical. The fact a 20-year-old enriches us from the start is a good sign. He's a top player, which is why many teams wanted him."

Another player signed by Madrid from Germany, Dani Carvajal joined the club from Bayer Leverkusen 10 years before Bellingham. The defender has won 25 major trophies, including a record six Champions Leagues titles with Los Blancos, and from day one identified his Bernabéu new team-mate as the real deal.

"He puts on his 'Superman' cape in nearly every game," he said. "But we don't want to deify him too much because the bar is set too high. From the first moment when he started training, we looked at each other, the veterans, and we said 'he knows what he's doing'. We saw that he's very fast, technically he's crazy, he's a finisher and he's very intelligent."

The Ancelotti Factor

He finds a way to let a lot of the boys play with freedom.

Bellingham's manager for his debut season at the Bernabéu, the veteran Italian coach played a pivotal role in the player's meteoric rise.

A modern managerial great, Carlo Ancelotti has won the league title in all of Europe's top five leagues during a trophy-laden career with AC Milan, Chelsea, PSG, Bayern Munich and Madrid. No manager can rival his five Champions League triumphs and during his second spell in the dugout with Los Blancos, rejoining the club in 2021, he has continued to collect silverware with reassuring regularity.

"It's difficult to compare two different generations."

The secret of the Italian's success, according to Bellingham, is simple. Ancelotti is a brilliant man manager and wherever he coaches, his teams never play with fear. To illustrate the philosophy, Bellingham tells a story from the dressing room inside the Etihad stadium before Madrid's second leg quarter-final Champions League clash with Manchester City. The tie was level at 3-3 after the first game and, away from home, Los Blancos dramatically went through after a penalty shootout.

"Before the game, I caught him yawning and asked him 'boss, are you tired?'" Bellingham said. "[He replied] you need to go out there and excite him. That's the calmness and confidence he brings to the team. He finds a way to let a lot of the boys play with freedom. One of our biggest strengths is that we're so off-the-cuff. All credit goes to him. He found the right position for me and gave more freedom, so now I'm flying."

Deploying the England star in a more advanced role in Spain was certainly a masterstroke by Ancelotti, the success of which worked better than even better than the manager himself could have predicted.

"Obviously it's a bit surprising, it's surprising everyone," Ancelotti admitted early in the season. "I don't think anyone could have imagined his adaptation

OPPOSITE: Carlo Ancelotti has been a key figure in Bellingham's emergence as a world-class player.

BELOW: Comparisons have been drawn between Bellingham and his childhood hero Zinedine Zidane.

to this style of football. He's been outstanding. He has plenty of personality and has adapted very quickly to the team's system. It seems like he's been with us for a long time and he's a very talented player. It feels like he is 30, for his character, his personality. He's always focused, he knows what he has to do. That's strange for a player who's just 20. And then the quality he has, the physical strength."

By the time Bellingham's unforgettable double saw Madrid win El Clasico against Barcelona at the Nou Camp in October, his manager was convinced of the youngster's potential. "He can easily reach 20 to 25 goals," he said.

"We don't have in mind that he is a scorer or a striker. Bellingham plays like a veteran. He's got a fantastic attitude. We didn't want a draw and his equaliser changed the dynamic of the game. Bearing in mind that he's had to adapt to our club, to a new culture and language, he's done very well. For us, obviously he's the best."

When talk of Bellingham as the new Zinedine Zidane began, Ancelotti however was quick to lower expectations of a player still so early in his career. "It's difficult to compare two different generations," he said. "What I see is his ability to get into the box. Zidane didn't have that. And the individual quality which Zidane had, Bellingham doesn't have yet."

In action in the Madrid derby, Bellingham proved his credentials with his new club with spectacular speed.

The Champions League final was a triumphant climax to a brilliant debut season for the midfielder.

Bellingham built a strong rapport with the Madrid fans after swapping Germany for Spain.

INSET BELOW: Bellingham has been all over the Spanish newspaper headlines.

KEPA, CERCA DE LLEGAR CEDIDO

MARCA

0 2

UN JUGADOR COMO UNA CATEDRAL

BELLINGHAM SE ESTRENA EN LALIGA CON UNA EXHIBICIÓN

El inglés se adueña de San Mamés y marca el segundo gol • Rodrygo abre el marcador • La lesión de Militão, lo peor para el Madrid

21:30

EL BARCELONA, PENDIENTE DE LAS INSCRIPCIONES

Dembélé ya es del PSG

ÉXITO DE UNA GENERACIÓN

Alcaraz: el fin de una racha

21:30

Partidazo para cerrar el Torneo del Centenario

SUPERCOPA 'HAT-TRICK' DE DANI OLMO AL BAYERN EN EL ESTRENO DE HARRY KANE

GUÍA MARCA YA A LA VENTA

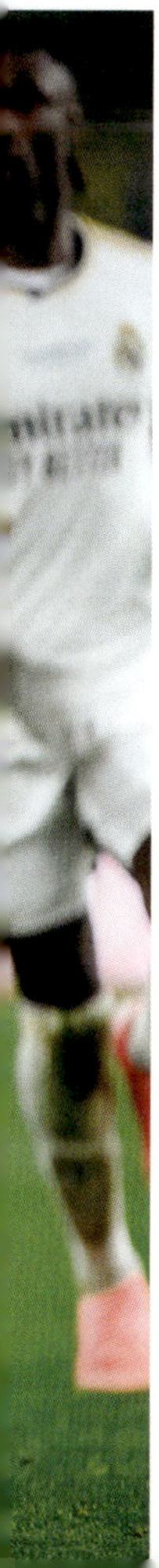

'HEY JUDE'

A club well accustomed to superstar signings, Real Madrid and its supporters quickly fell in love with Bellingham both on and off the pitch.

"He's called to mark an era here and be a future Real Madrid legend," said Florentino Pérez, the Real president, when the young Englishman was officially unveiled as the club's latest recruit. "I want to give you our thanks as you have done everything possible so that you could achieve your dream and become a 'Madridista' and for having the ambition of continuing your story at this club. He could have gone to any other team but he chose to be here. At only 20, he is one of the best in the world."

It was praise indeed from the man responsible for bringing legends such as Zinedine Zidane, Cristiano Ronaldo and Karim Benzema to the Bernabéu in the past and when the ceremony to introduce Bellingham was over, the fans waited expectantly to see if the hype was justified.

It did not take long for them to get their answer and after his goalscoring debut in August against Athletic Bilbao, the Spanish media were universally agreed Los Blancos already had a new hero. "Bellingham is the Boss," ran the headline in the *AS* sports newspaper while *La Liga TV* added the midfielder "has already won the hearts of the fans, they say he was born to play for Real Madrid and they never say this except for the very best talents."

In his post-match interview Bellingham spoke at first in Spanish to increase his popularity with the Bernabéu faithful even further. "Primer partido, primer victoria y primer gol," he said. "Hala Madrid." In English, it was "first match, first victory and first goal. Go Madrid."

RIGHT: Madrid president Florentino Pérez was determined to sign Bellingham despite the youngster's relative inexperience.

After he scored an unforgettable solo goal in the Champions League against Napoli in October, the *Mundo Deportivo* newspaper joined the fan club. "He is half artist, half warrior," it said. "Bellingham has been the signing of the summer. He slipped through the Napoli defence like a knife through butter. The Englishman has become an idol with his goals and good play."

The reaction of the fans was summed up in a single tweet: "Bellingham could honestly go down as one of the best signings ever, not just of the season," it said. "This form is absolutely incredible."

As the goals and match-winning performances continued, Bellingham's name soon began to be mentioned in the same breath as the legendary players who had grace the Bernabéu before him. "His dream was always to be part of La Liga at the biggest level and he believes he belongs to that level," Spanish football expert Guillem Balagué told the BBC. "The comparisons have started, first Zidane, then [Alfredo] Di Stefano. Everybody, all the players, are saying what a brilliant guy and brilliant footballer he is. He is the best player in the world right now."

By June, Bellingham's love affair with the Madrid faithful was in no doubt. Los Blancos had just won the Champions League at Wembley, sealing a famous La Liga and European double, and after the final whistle the home of football echoed loudly to the sound of the traveling fans serenading their star with The Beatles' classic Hey Jude.

ABOVE: The midfielder's natural talent, modesty and intelligence made him immediately popular with the supporters, press and club hierarchy.

YOUNG LION

AN ENGLAND YOUTH PLAYER AGED JUST 13, BELLINGHAM SHONE FROM THE START AS HE EMBARKED ON HIS UNSTOPPABLE MARCH TOWARDS THE SENIOR SIDE.

"My role models were Wayne Rooney and Steven Gerrard."

Like many aspiring young players, Bellingham's first memory of international football was watching his Three Lions heroes on television. Dreaming of following in their footsteps and wearing the famous white shirt is not unusual for countless youngsters up and down the country but for Bellingham those early days of seeing his idols in action conjured up mixed feelings.

"My role models were Wayne Rooney and Steven Gerrard because they played in England," he said. "I always remember watching the England games with my family. They weren't great times for England to be fair. I remember going out to Iceland [at Euro 2016], losing to Italy [at the 2014 World Cup], and that was probably my two earliest memories. So not the best memories from the perspective of an England fan. But it was really also fun, experiencing that with my brother, and always saying to each other that one day we'll be there."

He did not have to wait long for that dream to become a reality. In December 2016 the 13-year-old was called into the Under-15 squad and made his international debut against Turkey at St George's Park, the England HQ in the Midlands. Bellingham kept a diary for the Priory School website, detailing the biggest moment in his career so far. "My eyes lit up when I saw my very own England kit laid out perfectly," he wrote. "The surreal feeling of my studs digging into the grass wearing an official England shirt had to be put aside in exchange for concentration for the job at hand. Elation was the only word I could use to describe a truly fantastic day."

Between 2016 and 2018, Bellingham made eight appearances for the Under-15s in total, scoring once, and there was no doubt the quality of footballers he was now playing alongside accelerated his already rapid development. When England faced Belgium at St George's Park in 2017, for example, the Birmingham teenager lined up with Chelsea stars-in-waiting Cole Palmer and Noni Madueke, as well as future Bayern Munich attacking midfielder and German international Jamal Musiala.

By the end of 2018 he had graduated to the Under-16 set-up. Bellingham played 11 times, captained the side and scored four goals and the following year he was promoted to the Under-17s and selected by new manager Kevin Betsy to travel with the squad to Poland to compete in the eight-team Syrenka Cup in September 2019. The young Three Lions' opening fixture was against Finland and Betsy handed him his debut from the bench. Bellingham seized his opportunity, scoring the third goal in a 5-0 victory, and he was handed the captain's armband for the next game, once again netting the third in a 4-2 win over Austria.

ABOVE: Manager Aidy Boothroyd gave Bellingham his Under-21 debut against Kosovo.

OPPOSITE: Bellingham has been an England player at every level since first representing the Under-15s in 2016.

England were through to the final against Poland. Bellingham led the side out at the Zabrze Arena and faced a far sterner challenge against the hosts than they had in the previous rounds and the game

> ***The young England stars however held their nerve in the resulting penalty shootout triumphing 3-1 from the spot.***

finished 2-2 after normal time. The young England stars however held their nerve in the resulting penalty shootout, triumphing 3-1 from the spot. "Kevin Betsy's side will feel as though they could've won it in the 90 minutes following a dominant second-half performance," the Football Association website reported. "Having been clawed back, England put in a stronger second-half display and finished the game strongly in the search for a late winner.

But despite good efforts from Jude Bellingham, who skilfully controlled the ball to beat a man and volley at goal only to see his effort saved, they just couldn't find a way through when it mattered."

What did matter was England were champions and Bellingham, still a year younger than the majority of his team-mates and opponents, had excelled again. He was named the Player of the Tournament in Poland and although by now Birmingham fans were all to aware of the teenager's talent following his senior debut for the Blues, his potential was becoming clear to a far wider audience.

The next step should have been England Under-18 and Under-19 football but Bellingham's incredible progress saw the midfielder fast tracked through the Three Lions ranks and in September 2020 he was called straight into the Under-21 set-up by manager Aidy Boothroyd for the 2021 European Championship

RIGHT: The midfielder forced his way into the England Under-21 squad at the age of 17.

qualifiers against Austria and Turkey. His selection came two months after his headline-grabbing summer move to Borussia Dortmund and it was evident the England hierarchy now had high hopes for the teenager.

"The FA are planning an accelerated programme of development for the midfielder, who only turned 17 in June," wrote Rob Dorsett for *Sky Sports*. "The schedule is designed for him to be ready to join up with Gareth Southgate's senior squad in the next two or three years, depending on how he develops in Germany. If he gets as much game time as Jadon Sancho has in the past in the Bundesliga, there are even hopes Bellingham could be part of Southgate's plans for the 2022 World Cup in Qatar. However, there are concerns among some FA officials that pushing Bellingham too far too soon could be to his detriment. He has yet to be involved in a competitive international tournament with any of England's junior sides so there is also a desire for him to get that experience sooner rather than later."

Predictably there was nothing to worry about. A 62nd-minute substitute against Kosovo, Bellingham marked his first Under-21 cap with a late goal in a 6-0 demolition of the opposition to prove he was more than ready for his promotion. In making his debut, he made history as the youngest ever England Under-21 player.

There were to be only three more appearances for Boothroyd's side. By the end of 2020, Gareth Southgate had realised it was impossible to delay Bellingham's inevitable elevation to the senior squad any longer and in November he was selected among the substitutes for a friendly against the Republic of Ireland, the country he had been eligible to represent through his Irish grandfather, at Wembley. The game was 73 minutes old when the manager thrust the teenager into the fray. Aged 17 years and 136 days, he was the third youngest player ever to represent his country after Theo Walcott and Wayne Rooney and his senior England journey had begun.

His selection came two months after his headline-grabbing summer move to Borussia Dortmund.

"It is a requirement for a young player of that age to do a certain amount of education every day," said Southgate, revealing the debutant had had to juggle homework with training before winning his first cap. "So we have been helping him to fulfil that. I thought he was a little nervous at the start, which is completely understandable. It was such a big occasion. One of the hardest things is to fit in with the rest of the group. You are training and working with players who, in Jude's case, he has only seen from afar. But you could see the longer he got in and the more touches he got the more confident he got. It was a special moment for him and his family. It was exactly what we hoped to be able to give him – some training with the team, experience of working with top professionals and then a small taste of the game which will be really good for his development."

JUDE IN NUMBERS

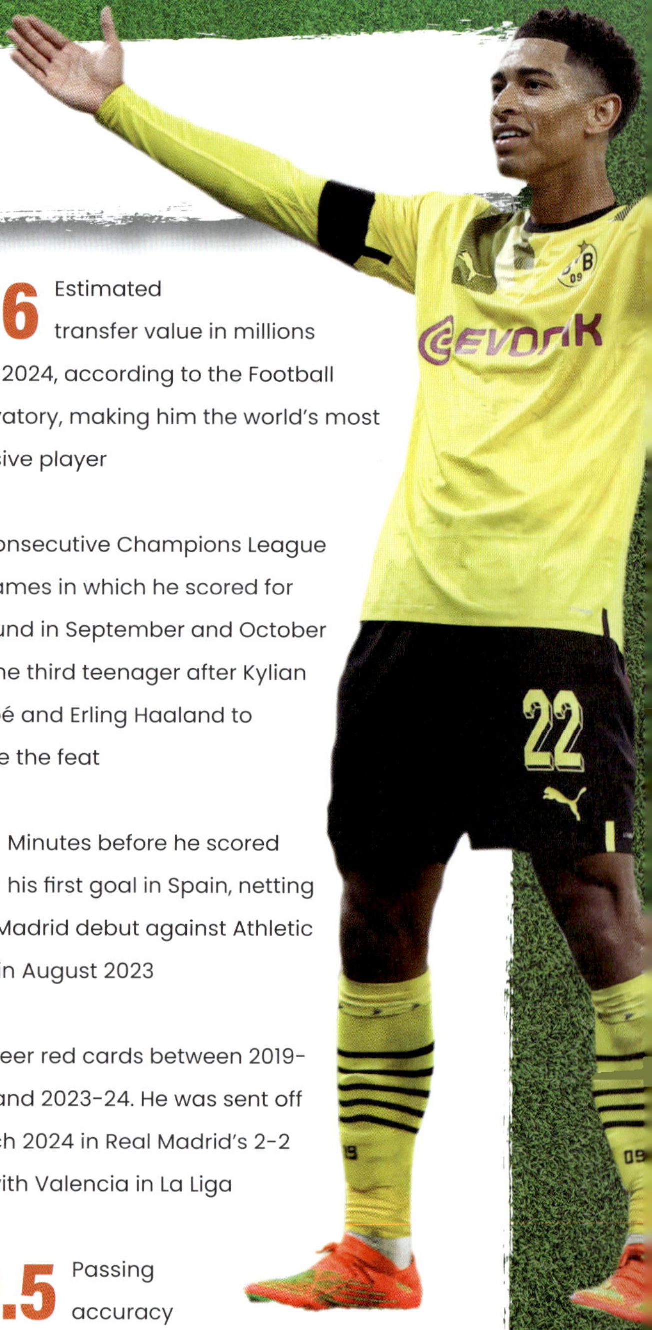

Here are the facts, figures and records behind the star's blockbuster first five seasons for club and country.

17 Minutes played on his senior England debut, coming off the bench at Wembley against the Republic of Ireland in November 2020

161 Combined league appearances for Birmingham, Dortmund and Madrid between 2019 and 2024 from a possible 186

7 Man of the Match awards during his debut 2023-24 campaign for Real Madrid

6,322 Age in days when he featured for Dortmund in the Champions League against Lazio in October 2020, breaking Phil Foden's record as the youngest English player ever to start in the competition

49 Combined goals and assists for Borussia Dortmund during his three seasons in Germany

2,324 Minutes on the pitch in La Liga in 2023-24

ABOVE RIGHT: Dortmund trademark celebrations.

OPPOSITE: Bellingham is a seasoned header of the ball.

236 Estimated transfer value in millions in May 2024, according to the Football Observatory, making him the world's most expensive player

4 Consecutive Champions League games in which he scored for Dortmund in September and October 2022, the third teenager after Kylian Mbappé and Erling Haaland to achieve the feat

37 Minutes before he scored his first goal in Spain, netting on his Madrid debut against Athletic Bilbao in August 2023

1 Career red cards between 2019-20 and 2023-24. He was sent off in March 2024 in Real Madrid's 2-2 draw with Valencia in La Liga

90.5 Passing accuracy percentage in the 2023-24 Champions League campaign, earning him the UEFA Young Player of the Season award

12 Winning streak in international football following his debut against Ireland in 2020. His first defeat in an England shirt came in his 13th game, against Hungary in Budapest in June 2022

1,257 Players to have represented England before Bellingham's Three Lions debut

6 Headed goals scored in his five seasons of senior football

41 Championship games played during his first season of senior football for Birmingham City in 2019-20

186 Height in centimetres

21 Total domestic cup competition appearances in England, Germany and Spain up to the end of the 2023-24 season

100,000 Replica Madrid shirt sales in the first four months after Bellingham signed for Madrid

13 Assists in his debut season in Spain in all competitions

74.25 Average number of touches per game in his three years in the Bundesliga

176 Senior career club appearances in all competitions for Birmingham and Borussia Dortmund, scoring 28 goals, before he had celebrated his 20th birthday

2.3 Average shots per game for Los Blancos in La Liga in 2023-24

10 Shirt number for England for the 2024 European Championship in Germany

220,000 Reported weekly wage at Real Madrid as part of his £11.4 million per year deal

32.5 Top speed in kph according to UEFA during 2023-24 Champions League

92 Bundesliga appearances as a teenager, a German top-flight record

3 Career penalties scored, converting from the spot for Dortmund against Hanover and Borussia Mönchengladbach and for Madrid against Almería

24 England caps as a teenager, all of which came as a Dortmund player – his first international appearance as a 20-year-old came against Ukraine in September 2023

1,900 Total minutes on the pitch for the Three Lions in his 29 games before the start of Euro 2024

A STAR IS BORN

ENGLAND HAD ALWAYS HOPED BELLINGHAM WOULD BE READY TO PLAY AT THE WORLD CUP IN QATAR IN 2022 AND, HANDED THE GREATEST OPPORTUNITY OF HIS FLEDGLING CAREER, THE TEENAGER DID NOT DISAPPOINT.

The list of iconic footballers to never have appeared in the beautiful game's biggest international tournament is a long one and although Bellingham's talent and tenacity had forced him into the England reckoning before he had turned 18, there was no guarantee he would make the squad for the 22nd edition of the competition in Qatar in 2022. He would still be a teenager when the Middle East welcomed the world's best teams for the first time and few players of such similarly tender years had ever been involved with England in a previous World Cup.

His first significant chance to press his claim for selection came in the 2020 European Championship finals. Delayed until the summer of 2021 due to Covid-19 travel restrictions, the tournament was staged across 11 countries for the first time and although Bellingham's game time was limited to 55 minutes in three appearances from the bench, the experience of being involved with the squad in the summer was invaluable to his development. The Three Lions' impressive progress to the final meant the youngster was in camp for over a month and his prolonged exposure to elite European football only served to hone his skills and focus.

Despite his relatively peripheral role in terms of minutes on the pitch, he nonetheless made headlines when he replaced captain Harry Kane late in the second half of the side's opening 1-0 group stage victory over Croatia. It was only his fifth cap but in taking the pitch aged 17 years and 349 days, Bellingham became the both the youngest Englishman to feature in a major tournament and the youngest player of any nationality to play in the European Championship. His latter record however was broken just six days later when Poland's Kacper Kozlowski played against Spain.

He made his second and third substitute appearances in the group phase against Scotland

His selection was one greeted by widespread excitement.

OPPOSITE: **Bellingham tasted tournament football for the first time at the finals of the 2020 European Championship.**

BELOW: **The midfielder was on the scoresheet in the 2022 World Cup in a 6-2 demolition of Iran.**

and then the Czech Republic but had to be content with a watching brief from the dugout as the Three Lions beat Germany, Ukraine and Denmark in the knockout stages before the agony of losing to Italy on penalties at Wembley in the country's first ever appearance in the European Championship final.

There were just 18 months between the Euros and the World Cup and the jury was still out whether he would make the cut. The midfielder started two of the Three Lions' 10 qualifying matches, coming off the bench in two more fixtures, but when Gareth Southgate ultimately unveiled his 26-strong squad for the finals, Bellingham's name was on the list. The youngster would be one of only a handful of teenagers among the 832 players from 32 competing countries in Qatar and his selection was one greeted by widespread excitement in the media.

"The Birmingham boy has been tearing it up at Borussia Dortmund for some time," said the *Mirror*. "With Jordan Henderson entering his final years and Kalvin Phillips far from 100 per cent, Bellingham must partner Declan Rice in midfield. And that will make England far more dynamic. A bidding war is expected to commence next summer and his performances over the next couple of weeks could drive him and the fee to new heights."

The Three Lions opened their campaign in late November at the Kalifa International Stadium against Iran and Bellingham did indeed start the Group B

clash, his first in a finals fixture. The midfielder was unsurprisingly far from overawed by the magnitude of the occasion and in the 35th minute announced himself at the tournament in style, rising above the defence to head Luke Shaw's cross into the far top corner for the opening goal. England went on to win 6-2 and Bellingham's contribution was not finished, playing a key part in Raheem Sterling's third and Jack Grealish's sixth for Southgate's side.

His goal was the first of his international career and made him England's second youngest goalscorer in the World Cup behind Michael Owen, who was on target against Romania in France 24 years earlier. It also introduced the vast global audience watching to his trademark goal celebration for the first time.

ABOVE: Bellingham's opening goal came after 35 minutes in the group stage clash with Iran in Qatar.

OPPOSITE: Wales were dispatched 3-0 at the World Cup to secure the Three Lions' place in the knockout stage.

His stunning debut in the tournament left the watching pundits struggling to find superlatives to sum up his performance. "We talk about the great midfielders that we've played with and seen in England in our generation – but none of them were

> *"The authority that he plays with on the pitch goes well beyond his years."*

doing what he's doing at this age, on this stage," said England legend Rio Ferdinand. "The authority that he plays with on the pitch goes well beyond his years. He's a fabulous footballer but to deliver at a World Cup like that at that age is incredible." Striker Alan

Shearer, who scored 30 goals in 63 appearances for the Three Lions, was equally impressed. "It was a

"It was a complete performance from a really exciting player."

complete performance from a really exciting player," he said. "It had everything, he put in the tackles, the work-rate, his passing was superb, he got his goal, it really was a special day for him."

There was no about the teenager's selection for the next game after the Iran match and he duly lined-up in the starting XI to play the USA four days later. It was a tough and frustrating 90 minutes against the Americans in Al Khor and England were unable to book their place in the knockout stages with a game to spare after being held to a goalless draw. A British derby against Wales was their final group assignment at the Ahmad bin Ali Stadium in front of 44,000 fans and with qualification not yet secured, the stakes were high. Bellingham won his 20th cap and was one of only six of the starting XI to play the full 90 minutes and with the Three Lions dominant in midfield, they coasted to a 3-0 success to extend their stay in Qatar.

Now at the make-or-break stage of the tournament, England's Last 16 opponents were a dangerous Senegal side, the reigning Africa Cup of Nations champions, and despite being the most junior member of the side Southgate sent out to play, Bellingham was simply magnificent in the middle of the park. His first memorable contribution came seven minutes before half time when he surged

"With him in the team, the sky is the limit."

purposefully forward onto a pass from Harry Kane and as three defenders desperately tried to shut him down, he produced an inch-perfect, left-footed delivery to Jordan Henderson who was unmarked in the box and had the simplest tasks to stroke home for England's opener.

His second match-turning intervention came in first-half injury time. Senegal were threatening to equalise until Bellingham stormed out of his own area and broke up the attack and then sprinted with the ball at feet into the opposition half, cutting a gaping hole through a defence that was now in disarray.

OPPOSITE: The Madrid star was in the starting XI for England's Last 16 showdown with Senegal.

BELOW: In the thick of the action, the Three Lions stormed to a 3-0 win over the Senegalese.

Unselfishly he laid off to Phil Foden, who in turn set up Kane to make it 2-0. Bellingham's pivotal role in the goal showcased all of his pace, poise and vision simultaneously and effectively settled the contest. His set-up for Henderson made him the first teenager to provide an assist in the knockout stages of a World Cup since records began.

England were ultimately 3-0 winners and the reaction to the Dortmund star after the game was universally positive. Voted the Player of the Match by the readers of the *BBC Sport* website, he was also lauded by former England defender Martin Keown on the broadcaster's coverage of the game. "Different class," he said. "Best performance I have seen from a midfield player in this competition. When I look back to the last World Cup, it feels like our midfield has improved most of all and Bellingham is a major part

of that. He is a top-level player and we are lucky to have him. With him in the team, the sky is the limit."

The written press were no less impressed by his skilled, all-action display. "A perfect 10 for majestic Jude Bellingham," said the *Evening Standard*. "Bellingham became the youngest player to start a knockout tournament game for England since Wayne Rooney in 2004. The 19-year-old was a dominant force at the heart of the midfield and has already emerged as England's most important player. Absolutely sensational." *The Guardian* added: "What a talent. Pressed, set up Henderson's goal before brilliantly sparking the move for England's second." According to *The Independent*, he was "England's driving force and [it was] another sublime performance from the 19-year-old on the World Cup stage."

Reigning world champions France stood between the Three Lions and a place in the semi-finals in Qatar. A capacity crowd of 69,000 descended on the Al Byat stadium to witness the 32nd meeting between the two sides and the latest instalment of the Anglo-French clash was nothing if not dramatic. The French took an early, first-half lead but after the break Bellingham came agonisingly close to a spectacular equaliser when he unleashed a fierce volley from outside the box which produced an equally spectacular, acrobatic tip over the crossbar from goalkeeper Hugo Lloris.

The young star however continued to surge forward and was instrumental in England's equaliser. Finding space in the French penalty area, Bellingham produced a beautiful interchange with Bukayo Saka,

receiving the ball from the Arsenal forward before instinctively backheeling it to him. Their link-up caused panic in the defence and Saka was brought down, skipper Kane stepping up to smash home the penalty and in the process equal Wayne Rooney's record of 53 international goals.

There was 12 minutes remaining when France scored again through an Olivier Giroud header but Bellingham was unbowed and it was his superb long-range pass that earned England a second penalty after Mason Mount was fouled. This time however Kane uncharacteristically blazed his spot kick over the French bar and there was not enough time for Southgate's side to salvage a draw and send the quarter-final into extra-time.

England's exit was heartbreaking but the tournament had been a personal triumph for Bellingham. Still only in his fourth season as a professional, he started all five of England's games and played 415 of the 450 minutes the team were on the pitch. His goal against Iran and Man of the Match display against Senegal were the highlights rather than the full story of his contribution in Qatar and the teenager's class, energy and maturity were evident throughout the campaign.

"I'm confident I can achieve the things I want to achieve."

OPPOSITE: Defeat to France in the quarter-finals of the World Cup was a bitter pill to swallow.

BELOW: Bellingham only enhanced his international reputation in Qatar in 2022 despite the team's exit.

"Bellingham was one of the most sought-after midfielders in Europe before the tournament began,

> *"He was stunning in the opening game and brilliant against Senegal."*

but now the hype has reached a totally new level." said *Planet Football* after England's elimination. "This was the tournament where he came of age," said the *Mirror's* chief football writer John Cross. "He was stunning in the opening game and brilliant against Senegal, when he took the game by the scruff of the neck. A future England captain."

For the player himself, the World Cup was an experience which left him with mixed feelings but ultimately positivity about his own and England's future.

"We had a tournament that the country can be proud of," he said. "We put up a really strong fight against one of the best teams in the world. We went out narrowly and you learn to use it as ammunition for the next ones, and that's how I've taken it. I was really proud of it. But you can't be satisfied because you go with the intention of winning it and I really did feel like we had the chance to, especially after we got through against Senegal. Had we beaten France and gone through, who knows what can happen? I personally enjoyed the kind of pressure of the games and the responsibility that the manager gave me. I think you can create pressure for yourself through lack of preparation and confidence. Luckily, I don't lack confidence and I always try to stay prepared. I'm confident I can achieve the things I want to achieve. You come to terms with it pretty quickly, but I still think about it at times.

"There was an instance in training where I had a shot and I thought, that was just like the one that I had in the France game, and if I put it more to the left, would we have gone through? I was involved in the first penalty where I flicked it to Bukayo [Saka], and the second one, when I put the pass behind to Mason [Mount]. I always think, what if I'd just put it on Mason's toe and he went and scored? Then there would have been no second penalty. You can overthink things, but I think you come to terms with it quickly because you can't change it, whether you like it or not. Then you're on the plane home and think, we gave everything."

The game's first ever winter World Cup meant there was only a brief break from international football for Bellingham and he was wearing white again in Euro 2024 qualifying action just three months after returning to Dortmund from the Middle East. Under intense scrutiny, his performances in Qatar had seen him make a faultless transition from young talent to Three Lions regular and for a player who had progressed from being embroiled in relegation dogfight in the Championship in 2020 at age of 16 to the pinnacle of the worldwide game in 2022, the sky was now the limit.

In action against the United States in Al Khor, Bellingham featured in all five of England's World Cup outings.

The World Cup gave the star the biggest stage of his career so far.

The game against Senegal in 2022 in Qatar was only 21st appearance for his country.

THREE LIONS UNITED

Since breaking into the national team, Bellingham has lined-up with a golden generation of new and older players who have put England back on the football map.

It takes 11 outstanding players and a bench bursting with talent to make a great team. Many successful sides have boasted a single, shining star but without the collective efforts of a group, both on and off the pitch, even the most gifted of footballers will struggle at international level. Bellingham has made his own luck with England when it comes to his individual performances but he has also been blessed with some incredible team-mates.

The attacking trio of Bellingham, Phil Foden and Bukayo Saka was a constant for the Three Lions during Euro 2024 and the three player's England careers are remarkably similar. When Bellingham won his first cap as a replacement against the Republic of Ireland in November 2020 Saka was in the starting line-up, winning his second cap.

ABOVE: Bellingham has forged a productive partnership with Arsenal star Bukayo Saka whilst on England duty.

OPPOSITE: England captain Harry Kane has been an ever present since Bellingham made his Three Lions debut.

Foden was on the bench, also making his second appearance for his country as a second-half substitute for Jack Grealish.

Since that friendly, they played 111 times between them for England up to and including the European Championship final in Berlin and in the process forged an increasingly close relationship on international duty. "He [Bellingham] has so much quality," Saka said during the Euros in Germany. "He's so young but the talent he possesses is unbelievable. He can do everything in that middle, he can drive with the ball, he's aggressive. He is a really special player."

The sentiment was echoed by Foden. "He is one of the most gifted players I've ever seen," the Man City playmaker said at the World Cup in 2022. "I don't

want to big him up too much because he is still young but he's one of the most talented players I have ever seen. He has no weakness in his game. I think he will be the best midfielder in the world."

Both Saka and Foden are of the same generation as the Real Madrid talisman, although the pair are both slightly older, but Bellingham's growing impact on the England set-up is reflected in the reactions of the squad's more experienced players.

"I think he's a fantastic player," said skipper Harry Kane after the midfielder's breathtaking bicycle kick against Slovakia in Germany. "He has everything with and without the ball, presses really well, gets around the pitch, tackles. With the ball he can run, he can take players on, he can play a through ball and as you saw today he was really important with our goal. I like Jude a lot, he's a really good person. He's mature for his age and he's got great leadership skills as well."

Newcastle defender Kieran Trippier won his 54th cap for England in the same game – a March 2021 World Cup qualifier against San Marino – as Bellingham played for only the second time for his country and watched his progress up close and from afar. "He doesn't seem like a 20-year-old," he said after the pair had both started in the 3-1 win over Italy in late 2023 that confirmed Euro 2024 qualification. "He is so mature for his age. Jude has pressure playing for Real Madrid and he has taken it in his stride. With the maturity, quality and aggression he's got, he's frightening."

EURO HEARTACHE IN BERLIN

FEATURING IN HIS SECOND EDITION OF THE EUROPEAN CHAMPIONSHIPS BEFORE HIS 21ST BIRTHDAY, BELLINGHAM RETURNED TO GERMANY IN 2024 DESPERATE TO END ENGLAND'S LONG AND AGONISING WAIT FOR MAJOR SILVERWARE.

When Gareth Southgate named Bellingham in his squad for Euro 2020, played out a year late due to Covid-19, it was a bold decision. The teenager had just four caps and only one international start for his country ahead of the tournament but the manager had faith and, not for the first time in his career, Bellingham made history when he came off the bench in the Three Lions' group phase clash against Croatia at Wembley. At 17 years and 349 days old, he became the youngest player in the history of the competition.

After his breathtaking, double-winning debut season for Real Madrid in 2023-24, Bellingham's selection three years later was never in doubt. After an energy-sapping 47 games for club and country over the season, he joined up with the England squad late following victory in the Champions League final to give him time to rest body and mind but once he returned to the fold, his and the collective focus was clear. England had fallen at the final hurdle in 2021, losing to Italy on penalties in the final, and with what was widely regarded as an even more talented squad, hopes were high the team was now ready to take the next step under Southgate and lift the trophy.

ABOVE: Bellingham had limited time to train with the rest of the England squad before the Euro 2024 finals in Germany.

ABOVE RIGHT: Bellingham announced himself at the tournament in spectacular style with an unstoppable header against Serbia.

The Three Lions began their bid for glory against Serbia in the Arena AufSchalke in Gelsenkirchen. After three substitute appearances in the previous tournament, Bellingham started a European Championship match for the first time and he marked the occasion in typically emphatic style. The game was a mere 13 minutes old when the midfielder engineered an attack, passing to Kyle Walker on the right. The full-back opened up the Serbian defence with an incisive pass to Bukayo Saka, who delivered

the cross. Bellingham arrived in the area like a runaway train and with his potent mix of power, anticipation and sheer determination, he outmuscled his marker to score with an unstoppable diving header from the edge of the six-yard box. It proved to be the only goal of the game and England were, crucially, up and running with a 1-0 victory.

> ***He outmuscled his marker to score with an unstoppable diving header from the edge of the six-yard box.***

"The goal comes from a great movement between some great players," he said after the game. "Those magic moments where it comes together so naturally are really nice. I try to just keep making [the runs into] the box because I know players can find me and I know I can deliver."

It was Bellingham's 30th cap for the Three Lions and, his match-winning goal aside, a momentous one. At 20 years and 353 days, the Madrid star became the youngest ever European footballer to have played at three major finals following his appearances at Euro 2020 and the World Cup in Qatar two years later. From an England perspective, he had eclipsed Michael Owen's previous record of 22 years and 170 days old while the great Cristiano Ronaldo was 23 years and 123 days old when he had achieved the milestone.

Unsurprisingly he was named Man of the Match in Gelsenkirchen and his overall performance was met with universal and glowing praise by the media.

ABOVE: Bellingham celebrates England's opening goal at Euro 2024 with team-mate Trent Alexander-Arnold.

OPPOSITE: Waving to the crowd after starring for England in the match against Serbia.

"The combination of power and grace in that No. 10 shirt had echoes of the game's most complete players in his position," said *Sky Sports*. "A drop of the shoulder here, a driving run there. Time and again, he received the ball in tight areas and opened up

"The combination of power and grace in that No. 10 shirt had echoes of the game's most complete players in his position."

space for himself with ease. Harry Kane is the England captain, his country's record goalscorer, but this is Bellingham's team now. While Kane stayed high, having the fewest touches of the ball of any England player in the opening 45 minutes, Bellingham had the most. He was dominant.

"On the ball, he oozed class. A gorgeous cross-field volley drew gasps followed by admiring calls of 'Jude' from the England supporters among the crowd. He completed the most passes in the final third and

"He was fouled twice as often as anyone else in the first half and those were just the ones that the referee stopped play for."

ranked second for dribbles. Serbia could not stop him by fair means or foul. He was fouled twice as often as anyone else in the first half and those were just the ones that the referee stopped play for. At one point, he rose from the deck in one movement to glide away all the same.

"Off the ball, he was just as impressive, leading the press. Nobody else won more than four duels in that first 45 minutes. Bellingham won *eight*. There was a

"On the ball, he oozed class."

feistiness too, epitomised by his trademark rousing of the crowd before squaring up to an opponent. If there is an issue around mentality, in this squad or even in the national psyche, he is unaffected by it. At club level, the accepted wisdom is that Real Madrid possess an innate belief others lack. Bellingham carries that same swagger in an England shirt.

"How far can it carry the rest? England as a team will need to improve. If they can do so, they know they have a player in Bellingham who looks ready to grab hold of this tournament and make it his own. 'He writes his own scripts', said Southgate afterwards. This was only the first chapter, but it was special."

Four days later England faced Denmark in Cologne. The clash saw Kane open the scoring for the Three Lions with a close-range left-footed finish in the 18th minute but the Danes equalised 11 minutes before half time and Southgate and his side ultimately had to settle for a share of the points. It was a similar story in their final group game against Slovenia in Cologne but while the performance in a goalless draw in front of 41,000 fans was far from stellar, another point was enough to seal top spot in Group C and ensure the Three Lions were safely through to the knockout stages.

England were the hot favourites to beat Slovakia in the Last 16 but few could have predicted the dramatic and last-gasp nature of what was ultimately a 2-1 triumph. Bellingham turned 21 the day before the match, which saw the Three Lions return to Gelsenkirchen, but whatever modest celebrations he had enjoyed to celebrate his birthday were eclipsed by the delirious

scenes inside the Arena AufSchalke as the midfielder kept the dream of reaching the final alive.

There was a stunned silence in the stadium when Slovakia scored the opening goal after 25 minutes of the first half. Silence began to slowly turn to dissatisfaction as England tried to find the equaliser but as the clock ushered in the second half, the Three Lions still trailed and anxiety and frustration were the dominant emotions in the crowd.

When Declan Rice hit the right-hand post with 10 minutes left, it seemed England were heading home prematurely but Bellingham refused to accept defeat and stepped forward with a pivotal moment of pure genius. The game was 94 minutes and 34 seconds old when the Three Lions won a throw-in deep into injury time in the Slovak half. Walker prepared to unleash an all-or-nothing long delivery and as his throw sailed into the box, centre-back Marc Guéhi

ABOVE: Bellingham's wonder goal against Slovakia saved England and lit up the tournament.

OPPOSITE: The Madrid midfielder was on target in a tense penalty shootout victory over Switzerland in the quarter-finals.

was the first to the ball with his head, glancing the ball backwards further into the danger area. The crucial flick found its way to Bellingham. He had no time to control it and instead relied on instinct, producing a spectacular overhead bicycle kick from

England had only 86 seconds left to spare themselves from the humiliation of a defeat.

eight yards out. The midfielder caught it perfectly with his right foot and as it hit the back of the net, England had been handed an unbelievable late reprieve.

The Three Lions made the most of Bellingham's incredible intervention. Captain Kane scored with a

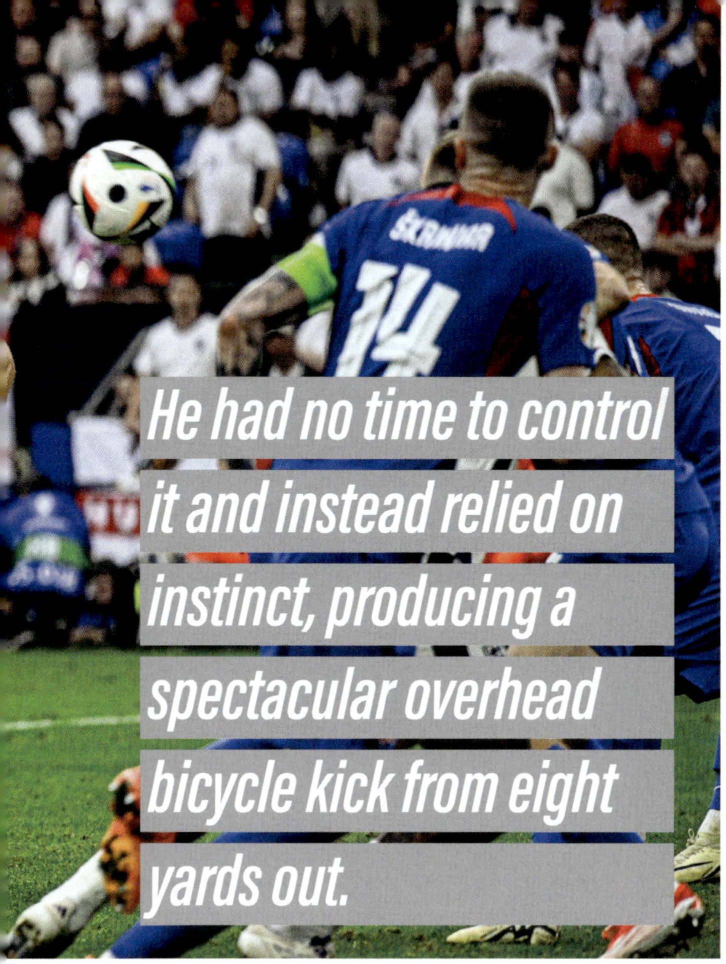

He had no time to control it and instead relied on instinct, producing a spectacular overhead bicycle kick from eight yards out.

thumping header in the second minute of extra time to give his team the lead and England held firm for what was left of the contest and book their place in the quarter-finals.

"England had only 86 seconds left to spare themselves from the humiliation of a defeat that would sit uncomfortably in the chamber of sporting horrors alongside the loss to Iceland at Euro 2016," said *BBC Sport*. "Failure to do so would surely have signalled the end of Gareth Southgate's time as England manager – it may still come irrespective of their fate in Germany – and a wide-ranging inquest into everything surrounding a mystifying failure to show up at Euro 2024. And then came Bellingham. In a flash of genius that will be replayed and talked about for years, Bellingham took off in an audacious show of athleticism and individual skill to send a stunning overhead kick past Slovakia keeper Martin Dubravka. He turned away, appearing to mouth 'who else?' Who else indeed?"

It was, according to Kane, a goal which ranked as "one of the best in our country's history" while the reaction to the score beyond the English press was equally glowing. "It was a goal where brilliance and beauty matched its importance," said the *New York Times*. "England were seconds from elimination when Bellingham showed poise and athleticism to add to his growing list of crucial strikes for club and country this season."

Nearly 17 million fans tuned in across the country to watch the team play Switzerland in Dusseldorf in the last eight. Hopes of a less nerve-jangling match and smoother progress in the tournament however did not materialise as the Three Lions once again had to dig deep to get the job done. The Swiss broke the deadlock in the 75th minute but while it had taken England over an hour to level against Slovakia, they were level only five minutes later in their quarter-final thanks to an eye-catching solo effort from Saka.

Extra-time failed to produce a decisive goal and it went to a penalty shootout. Substitute Cole Palmer scored the Three Lions first spot kick while keeper Jordan Pickford kept out Switzderland's opening effort. Bellingham was next up for the Three Lions and after a stutter step in his run-up, sending the Swiss keeper right, he clinically side-footed the ball into the bottom left corner. There were no more misses and when Trent Alexander-Arnold was emphatically on target with the fifth and final penalty, England were through to the last four.

> *He found the tireless Madrid midfielder, who produced another pinpoint lay-off under pressure for Palmer to stroke home a beautiful leveller with his left.*

More drama awaited them against the Netherlands in Dortmund. For Bellingham it was an emotional return to the Westfalenstadion where he had spent three successful seasons but there was no time to renew old friendships as the Three Lions prepared for the Dutch. It was England's toughest assignment yet and it became even harder after only seven minutes in the west of Germany when Holland scored with a stunning long-range shot. By now reluctantly familiar at coming from behind, the side rallied and equalised in the 18th minute after a controversial penalty awarded for a foul on Kane, the captain converting from the spot. England though struggled to find a way through the Dutch defence for a second time and 30 minutes of extra time seemed inevitable for a second successive match until substitute Ollie Watkins delivered the knockout blow in added time, scoring from the tightest of angles to seal victory.

The Three Lions were back in the final, three years after their defeat to the Italians, but this time it was Spain who stood between Southgate's side and a place in the history books as only the second England team to win a major title. The squad decamped to the capital Berlin and the city's famed Olympiastadion for the last, decisive match and potential glory.

It was goalless against the Spanish, the three-time European champions, at half time but many of those in the stadium had not yet returned to their seats when winger Nico Williams scored for Spain seconds after the restart. It was the fourth time in their four

LEFT: Bellingham watched as Cole Palmer scored the second-half equaliser in the Euro 2024 final against Spain

BELOW: The first final of his international career ended in defeat for Bellingham in Berlin.

knockout stage fixtures England had conceded the opening goal and for the fourth time the team found a way back into the game. Bellingham started the counter attack in the 73rd minute, laying off to Palmer inside his own half, who passed to Saka on the right. The forward raced down the line and looking up, saw Bellingham in the box. He found the tireless Madrid midfielder, who produced another pinpoint lay-off under pressure for Palmer to stroke home a beautiful leveller with his left.

The ecstasy of equalising was replaced with the agony of conceding the winner four minutes from the end. The late Spanish goal left the Three Lions precious little time to rally again and although Rice and Guéhi both had injury-time goal-bound headers blocked on the line, England could not produce yet another miraculous rescue act in Berlin. Bellingham's frustration on the touchline after the final whistle was obvious but when he spoke to the media, he was in a more philosophical frame of mind.

"To lose in that way is really cruel," he said. "We probably didn't play our best game, but there were definitely some good moments and we felt like we got back into the game, and then to be sucker-punched with the late goal, it's heartbreaking. We all wanted nothing more than to make history and to make the people of England proud and we never managed to do it, we didn't quite deliver."

It was not the fairytale ending to a record-breaking season for Bellingham for his club and then country but given the quick-fire nature of his international career, there will be many more chances for the 21-year-old in the future on the biggest stage.

Euro 2024 was a tournament of highs and lows for Bellingham and his England team-mates.

Bellingham and skipper Harry Kane scored five goals between them at the European Championship in Germany.

The midfielder and Spanish teenager Yamine Lamal represented the game's new generation at Euro 2024.

THE SOUTHGATE FACTOR

The man who handed Bellingham his England debut, Gareth Southgate moulded the midfielder's international career with spectacular results.

It is a brave manager who calls a 17-year-old into the Three Lions squad for the first time. Whatever the talents of the teenager, it is inevitably a gamble but one which Southgate did not come to regret after promoting Bellingham to the senior set-up in 2020. His first cap from the bench against the Republic of Ireland at Wembley was no more than a brief, second-half cameo but it was the beginning of his remarkably rapid transformation from international novice to automatic starter and veteran of three major tournaments.

From the start, Southgate has walked a fine line between overloading Bellingham with the weight of expectation and, at the same time, acknowledging his talent. When he named the young midfielder in his Euro 2020 squad, he made it clear he was not included simply to build his confidence. "We're not just taking him for the experience," he insisted. "He's going to be an important player for England. Just in training in the last couple of days, to have a 17-year-old, who wants to compete with senior players, not only has the technique, but the competitiveness and maturity. He's a hugely exciting player."

In contrast, three years later as the Three Lions finetuned their preparations for Euro 2024, the manager stressed England were not a one-player team despite Bellingham's prolific exploits at club level for Real Madrid. The midfielder was headline news after his first season in Spain but Southgate wanted to take the pressure off his player.

"I'm sure he is capable of handling the pressure but we are not putting everything on Jude," he said. "We've got a lot of good players and it is a collective thing to go and try and win this tournament. He is, of course, a player with fabulous mentality and will have a big impact on the whole group."

RIGHT: Gareth Southgate was Bellingham's England manager for the first 36 games of his international career.

OPPOSITE: Southgate selected the young midfielder for three major tournaments before his 21st birthday.

Deployed in a number of different positions by Southgate, who has repeatedly described him as "super professional", Bellingham blossomed for his country and although his first 17 caps did not yield a first goal, he rewarded his manager's faith with five in his next 15 appearances, three coming in tournament football. The closeness of the relationship between the two was in evidence after the Three Lions' heartbreaking defeat to Spain in the final of Euro 2024. With Southgate's future as England boss in doubt, Bellingham made it clear how he felt about his manager and his impact on the national team.

"He will always have my respect and my love," he said in Berlin. "I've got nothing but respect for Gareth giving me my debut, he made me feel very at home. He is someone who, in the last year or two, our relationship's gone a little past football, where I feel like I can open up to him a lot and I think that speaks volumes of the kind of man he is. If he stays, then I'll be even more determined to win something for him because he deserves it. Sometimes the numbers, the statistics and the records don't lie. He's been our most successful manager since 1966."

The day after Bellingham gave the interview, Southgate announced his eight-year reign encompassing 102 games was over. After a World Cup semi-final and back-to-back European Championship finals, as well as handing Bellingham all 36 of his England caps to date, the 53-year-old had stood down. A new era beckons for both Bellingham and the Three Lions.

Appendix:
Career Stats & Honours

Birmingham City (2019-20)

Appearances: **44**

Goals: **4**

Borussia Dortmund (2020–2023)

Appearances: **132**

Goals: **24**

Real Madrid (2023-24)

Appearances: **42**

Goals: **23**

England (2020–2024)

Appearances: **36**

Goals: **5**

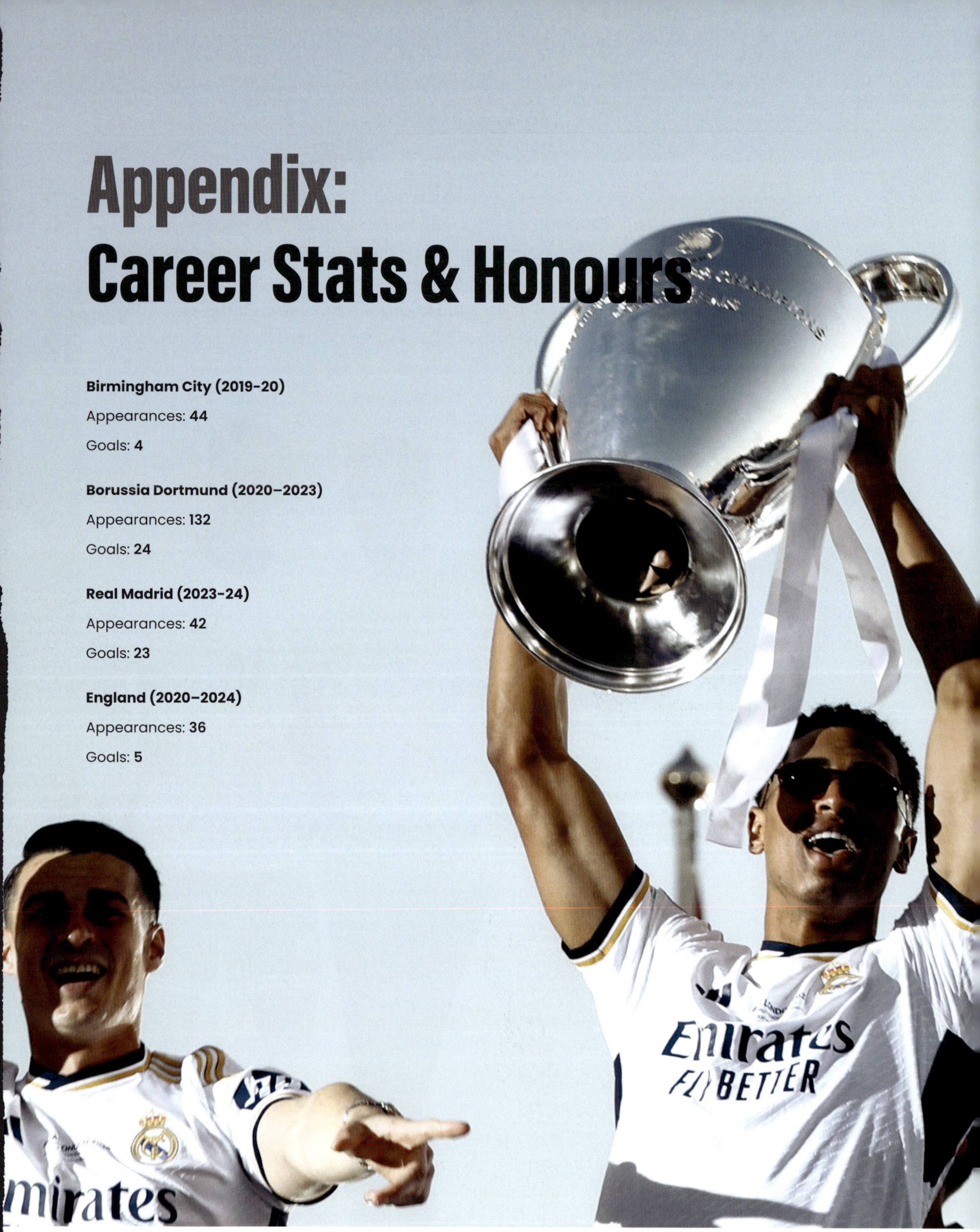

Honours

Borussia Dortmund

DFB-Pokal, **2020-21**

Real Madrid

La Liga, **2023-24**

Champions League, **2023-24**

Individual Awards

Birmingham City Young Player of the Year: **2019-20**

Football League Young Player of the Season: **2019-20**

Bundesliga Team of the Season: **2021-22, 2022-23**

Bundesliga Newcomer of the Season: **2020-21**

Kopa Trophy: **2023**

IFFHS Men's Youth World Team: **2021, 2022, 2023**

IFFHS Men's World's Best Youth Player: **2022, 2023**

ESPN Midfielder of the Year: **2022-23**

Bundesliga Player of the Season: **2022-23**

IFFHS Men's World Team: **2023**

Golden Boy: **2023**

Globe Soccer Awards Emerging Player of the Year: **2023**

FIFA FIFPRO Men's World 11: **2023**

La Liga Player of the Season: **2023-24**

La Liga Team of the Season: **2023-24**

Laureus World Breakthrough of the Year: **2024**

UEFA Champions League Team of the Season: **2023-24**

UEFA Champions League Young Player of the Season: **2023-24**

Bellingham became only the fifth British player to lift the Champions League with an overseas club in 2024.

Bellingham's 19 La Liga goals in 2023-24 were pivotal as Madrid were crowned champions of Spain for a 36th time.

The German Cup in 2021 was the first silverware of Bellingham's brief but bright Dortmund career.

EGO